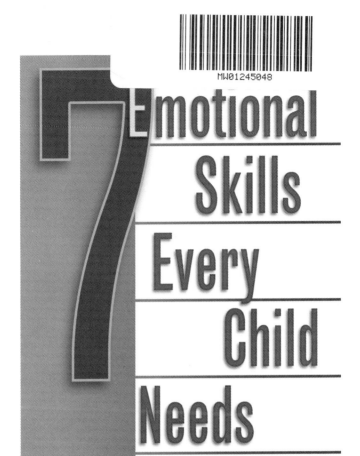

7 Emotional Skills Every Child Needs

Pam Galbraith & Rachel C. Hoyer

Beacon Hill Press of Kansas City
Kansas City, Missouri

ISBN 083-412-0496

Printed in the
United States of America

Cover Design: Ted Ferguson

Library of Congress Cataloging-in-Publication Data

Galbraith, Pam, 1958-
    7 emotional skills every child needs / Pam Galbraith and Rachel C. Hoyer.
        p. cm.
Includes bibliographical references.
    ISBN 0-8341-2049-6 (pbk.)
    1. Parenting—Religious aspects—Christianity. 2. Emotions in children—Religious aspects—Christianity. I. Title: Seven emotional skills every child needs. II. Hoyer, Rachel C., 1965- III. Title.

    BV4529.G35 2003
    248.8'45—dc21

                                                            2003007340

10 9 8 7 6 5 4 3 2 1

To Hannah, Erin, and Michael, you are my treasured reminders of how much the Father loves me.

And to Randy, thank you for your undying hope and love.

PRG

To Jeff, thanks for growing with me and encouraging me.

To Calista and Samuel, thanks for all you've taught me about love. I love you always and forever.

RCH

Contents

Introduction

O Lord, you have searched me and you know me. . . .
For you created my inmost being; you knit me together in my
mother's womb. I praise you because I am fearfully
and wonderfully made" (Ps. 139:1, 13-14).
"For we are God's masterpiece. He has created us anew
in Christ Jesus, so that we can do the good things he
planned for us long ago" (Eph. 2:10, NLT).

Chances are, you're reading this book because you have
young children, are expecting a child, or are anticipating
having children. So we'll take for granted that you value
children. But that's all we'll take for granted. I (Rachel) have
learned the hard way that not everything—including children—
comes easily.

When Jeff and I got married in 1992, we never dreamed having children would be difficult. Four years, many tests, several
surgeries, a miscarriage, and an ectopic pregnancy later, we
found ourselves facing infertility.

I'd just come out of surgery. The doctor had removed my
right fallopian tube—an ectopic pregnancy had ruptured it. My
left tube was not functional. The doctor came to talk to us, his
demeanor grave. He used words like "infertility" and "in vitro
fertilization." My mind shut him out. I could hear him, but I
was drawn to what I can only describe as a sort of vision. I saw a
long hallway, brightly lit and filled with doors. The doors nearest
me closed, then the rest began to close until there was only one
door left. I looked in that doorway and heard quite clearly, "Be
still, and know that I am God." A complete peace came over me.
This was God's plan for us. I tuned back in to the doctor's words.
He explained that everything else was working—we were just
without a transportation system to get fertilized eggs to the uter-
us. IVF could provide that transportation.

7

I'll spare you the details of the subsequent tests, doctor interviews, diagnoses and misdiagnoses, medications, ultrasounds, and teams of doctors and nurses. Suffice to say, we ended up in the hands of some of the best fertility doctors in the country and our first full round of IVF was successful. Our daughter, Calista, was born in November 1998. We had an unsuccessful round of IVF in November 1999. We tried again in 2001 and our son, Samuel, was born in January 2002. He and his sister are the joy of our lives.

Throughout our struggles to conceive children, I never asked God "Why me?" but I did ask Him, "What would You have me learn from this, Lord? And what am I to share with others about my experience?"

I think my father-in-law explained it best as he baptized my son. He said to Samuel, "In the coming years, when you ask why you were named Samuel Martin, we will tell you. The Martin part is obvious (it's Grandpa's name). But the Samuel is from the Bible, from the story of a woman named Hannah, who, like your mama, was told she couldn't have children. But Hannah must have been the first baby boomer, because she didn't take no for an answer. She sought medical help and, also like your mama, she prayed. Hannah prayed so hard the priest, Eli, thought she was either crazy or drunk. But Hannah didn't give up. And when God gave her a son, she named him Samuel, saying, 'The Lord has given me what I asked of Him, and now I give him back to the Lord.' (The name Samuel means 'God listens.')"

So every day when I look at my children, I am reminded that God has entrusted me with two most precious, most beautiful gifts and it's my job to "train them up" and give them back to Him. Are my children *more* precious because I went through so much to conceive them? To me, perhaps. But to God, they are as dear as all His children. Whether our children were conceived without a thought or through careful planning and medical intervention, they were *created* by God. He tells us He foreknew each of us. We are His workmanship, His masterpieces, formed by His very hands. I'm anxious to know what His plans are for Calista and Samuel. It took so much effort to get them here, I'm sure His plans for them must be marvelous.

The Parent Perspective

Recently in church, I (Pam) watched two sets of new parents dedicate their children to the Lord. They took vows that acknowledged their children as gifts from God. They agreed to raise them up "in the nurture and admonition of the Lord," and they acknowledged that each child was born for an individual purpose here on earth, ordained by God himself. It struck me. At that early point in my three children's lives, I hadn't thought about what purpose God would have for them. I only wondered about who they would become. The two perspectives are different. One involves our Creator directly; the other, indirectly. One view has God's perspective in mind while the other has a parent's dream for her child in mind. One view is limited, the other, infinite with possibilities.

If we were to survey new parents' perspectives about what they want most for their children when they grow up, they may say things like meaningful friendships, good marriages, success in a job. Many Christian parents would add a close relationship with Jesus Christ. That relationship with Christ has brought us comfort and security, so naturally we want the same for those we love.

God's Perspective

What is God's perspective? Perhaps all of those things—and more. If God has plans for our children before they are even born (Eph. 1:4-6 and Jer. 29:11); if He knits them together in the womb (Ps. 139:13); if He promises to equip them for the plans He has for them (Phil. 4:13); then that ought to be our vision too. What hope! His plans for our children far exceed ours, and He provides the way and means to accomplish the plan! He even gives us a major part in preparing our children for what's ahead. Basically, we have three God-given purposes for being alive.[1]

To Relate to God

First, we were created to relate to God. Gen. 2:7 says, "And the LORD God formed a man's body from the dust of the ground and breathed into it the breath of life. And the man became a living person" (NLT). But God didn't leave it at that. He invited us into fellowship with Him. When Jesus prayed for His disciples and all the believers for generations to come, He asked God, "that just as you are in me and I am in you, so they [all believers] will be *in us*" (John 17:21, NLT, emphasis added). He planned for us to be united with the Trinity. That word *in* suggests something intimate and close.

To Relate to Others

Second, we were born to relate to others. After God created Adam, He said, "'It is not good for the man to be alone. I will make a companion who will help him.' . . . Then the LORD God made a woman from the rib and brought her to Adam" (Gen. 2:18, 22, NLT). Clearly, God created us to need and want each other in every way. We are social creatures. The vast majority of us need interaction with others.

To Bear His Image

Last, we were created to bear the image of God. Gen. 1:27 says, "So God created people in his own image; God patterned them after himself; male and female he created them" (NLT). We bear the image of God as we relate to Him as Savior and Lord. God uses us to convince the world that He loves them. He cultivates the fruit of the Spirit in us for His kingdom's purposes.

Vision for the Task

It makes sense, then, to have vision going into this parenting thing. As you were growing up, did you have a coach or teacher who really believed in you? For me (Rachel) it was my high school speech and debate coach. Even when I thought I wasn't smart enough to compete in extemporaneous speaking, he told me I was. Because he spent time coaching me, teaching me, and believing in me, I worked hard. He believed in me and I wanted to do what he was sure I could. He saw potential I didn't know I had. On a much larger scale, God sees what each of us is capable of becoming. He sees us as transformed in spite of our failures. Think about that in terms of our children. If we believe that our children were born with a winning purpose ordained by God, then we'll see them as important to God. And if we recognize their importance in His kingdom, we'll fill them with love and hope and potential.

If, however, our scope is only as broad as getting them through the next 18 years with no noticeable rebellion or academic difficulties so they will eventually go to college, get jobs, marry, and live happily ever after, then we fail to see the bigger picture, including God's hope for them. Looking at parenting from God's perspective takes away some of the pressure for worldly success. But that doesn't mean our job is less important. Especially when it comes to our children's emotional and spiritual health and how they will relate to other people and to God, parenting with "God's perspective" is paramount.

Parents Matter

Simply by virtue of being a parent, you have power, prestige, and an exalted position in your child's eyes. You're the one who will meet his or her needs, provide comfort, care, and love. You have the privilege of preparing your child with skills that will help him or her be a better friend, spouse, coworker, and teammate. Your child will learn from you how to manage emotions, tell himself or herself the truth, care for others as well as self, put personal desires aside for the sake of what's best, have the tenacity to endure difficult and undesirable situations, and have hope.

There is a small window of opportunity in a child's life when his or her brain is best suited to begin learning basic emotional skills. As parents, we can do much in the early years to help our children manage their emotions and respond effectively to the feelings of others. It happens best when the brain is in full swing, developing billions of cells and pathways in its neural circuitry. These skills will not only improve your child's relationships with others but also help his or her physical health, academic achievement, personal success, and overall sense of well-being.[2]

You make a difference in your child's spiritual life too. Though we can't transmit our faith in God onto our children via osmosis, we awaken our child to God's love and call. It all happens through the parent-child connection, starting at that first meeting.

For Rachel, it was an ultrasound picture of her son when she was 30 weeks pregnant—a clear shot of his face. She actually recognized him from that picture when he was born. For me (Pam), it was the first time I held each baby. Like you, both of us marveled at their form and features, wondering what the next 18 years would hold. There is euphoria, an indescribable connection that happens in those first moments with your child. This emotion is a significant player in building the connection between parent and child.

Staying Connected

If you already have a child, you know the feeling. If you're anxiously awaiting your first child, you are in for the thrill of your life! After 30 hours of labor that ended in a C-section, I (Rachel) just wanted the whole experience of childbirth to be over. And I wanted to sleep! But when the doctor held my daughter up and said, "Mommy, it's a beautiful girl. Does she have a name?" all of the anguish, pain, and exhaustion melted away. I told him, "Yes. This is Calista." And I cried tears of joy. My husband was so giddy that he ran around the room hugging all the doctors and nurses. When the nurse handed Calista to Jeff, he was so immersed in his euphoria that he forgot to bring her over to me. When I finally got to hold her, I just wanted to drink her in, to hold her and hug her forever.

Here was this little creature and she knew me. She nestled in and sighed. She felt safe. She trusted me. That's a wonderful feeling—a bond built in part by emotion. And it's one that can be carried throughout the parent-child relationship.

But learning to keep that initial "love fest" going takes time and practice, patience and respect. It also requires an attitude of humility and forgiveness. From the beginning, a child's trust for his or her parent compels the child to cling to the parent and be taught. Some of the lessons are fun, others difficult. But through it all, parent and child have a chance to connect emotionally and truly enjoy each other.

I (Pam) watched from a distance a mother and son "connecting" at a summer Little League game. When Mom clapped for the team, she excitedly motioned for her smiling three-year-old to clap with her. Then she pulled him up on her lap, nestled her face in his neck, and held his hands so they could clap together. He giggled with delight, thoroughly enjoying these sweet moments with his mama. Variations on this theme continued for most of that short game. I thought, "Now that is a piece of heaven." It all looked so natural for them.

The next time I talked with this mother, I commented that she looked like she enjoyed her son. She said she does but that it was not always so. She told me she had to _learn_ how to be playful because it hadn't come naturally. She had a million things to think about and do each day, but near the top of her list was the desire to _enjoy_ her son. There's no doubt in his mind: He is loved and respected and enjoyed!

It starts with two people who _want_ to connect. Of course, your child is a willing participant: He or she needs you; you are his or her security. Your child needs you to show him or her how to live life to the fullest. With your encouragement and support, your child will learn to relax enough to trust you and let you lead along life's way.

We can almost hear some of you say, "Well, you are dead wrong about my kid! He came out of the womb yelling and hasn't quit!" The hardy resistance of a determined son or daughter ought to give you hope in these changing times. We need confident leaders for the future. Your strategic and persistent efforts at teaching your children will pay off. However, strategy requires knowing what you're up against.

Today's parents face several social conditions that can cause interference in even the best of "connections": a millennial mindset; prosperity; too little time.

Millennial Thinkers

Thirty-year-old Bret works in corporate America—in a big city with a high-paying job that affords him a comfortable home in the suburbs. When he interacts with coworkers, he shares his faith predominantly by example. He gently verbalizes his faith when someone experiences a crisis or when he's invited to give his opinion about current events. But it's risky. The common reaction is that Christianity is a crutch, outdated, even foreign.

For the most part, Bret's coworkers are young, aspiring businesspeople who have been turned off by religion. They are capable and successful on their own. They are healthy and living the lives they want. No need for a Savior. They are what we'd call *millennial* thinkers. In a nutshell, the millennial mind-set says:

There are no absolutes. Nobody is an authority on anything. And if there is a god, he or she is everybody's god—certainly not limited to only one way for salvation. What works for one millennialist may not work for another. Truth and reason are dubious. As a result, tolerance is a highly regarded virtue.

America should demand tolerance. We have become an angry, demanding society, crusading for victims everywhere while at the same time creating victims by throwing away truth and reason. Many people have become slaves to their addictions and appetites.

Americans are entitled to satisfy their desires. There is little reason or virtue in denying self-pleasure if you can afford it and are not hurting anyone else.

But the millennial mind-set also is curious about:

What lasts. They admire marriages that have lasted for decades. They are fascinated with great works that have been around hundreds of years and 17th-century saints who practiced solitude and other prayer forms antithetical to our busy lives.

What's real. Millennialists want a genuine product. They want to see us experience our faith, to know what's alive and working in our lives for everyday situations before they adopt it as their own. They don't want some superficial dogma that sounds nice on Sunday morning but is not applicable the other six and a half days of the week. And they are adept at discerning between true Christianity and what is false.

The millennial way of thinking has made Christian parenting difficult because we believe in several absolutes, including Jesus Christ as the only authority on truth. He is the only way to salvation. He has definite mandates for us to share with our children so we don't live as victims but rather as free men and women. And He wants us to know how to deny ourselves at times both for His and our own sakes. These truths go against the basic premises of millennial thinkers.

But because millennial thinkers want the real thing, they respect it when they think they see it. If your children experience a heavenly kind of grace in your home, and _see it work_, they are more likely to believe what you tell them about the source of that grace. They experience true Christianity.

Prosperity

Prosperity and affluence also make parenting different today. Please don't misunderstand—we're glad America has been prosperous. Prosperity can be a gift. But with it comes responsibility to manage it. America's baby boomers have been history's most indulged generation.[3] It's hard to believe, but we are indulging the next generation even more.

Thanks to social circumstances and media influences, Christian parents are tempted to give their children _stuff_ and opportunities. When the money's available in the family budget, it's hard to say no to those $150 tennis shoes. It's easy to hire someone to do the cleaning and excuse the kids from household chores. We wrestle with how much money and how many material things to give them and what to make them work for. And our children are in danger of suffering the same fallout we do—entitled, unbecoming attitudes and unmotivated work ethics. We are setting them up for insecurity when they finally live in the "real world."

Time

Ironically, parents now spend less time with their children. We work longer hours and are energy deficient, so we have difficulty parenting creatively and consistently. There are also more distractions. Cell phones, answering machines, caller ID, and E-mail, as efficient as they are, consume our time and keep life from remaining simple. We become consumed by time and how little of it we seem to have.

In the blazing summer of 2001, there were instances across the country where children died from being left in hot cars while their parents or caretakers went to work or were busy with something else.

One woman, whose children were saved by a passing police officer, complained that it took too much time to get her three children out of the car when she just had to run into the store for a minute. The tape on the news was astonishing. As her children were loaded into an ambulance, suffering from heat exhaustion and dehydration, she continued to justify her actions to the police officer. She was so consumed by the time she was saving, the gravity of the situation didn't sink in.

It's true—a lack of time makes it difficult to truly connect with our children. Our accelerated society has robbed us of the attention to detail and consistency necessary for effective parenting. But we need to take the *time* to look our children in the eye, get to know them, and teach them how to move in the right direction. It takes time to teach a child how to clean the bathroom and make it fun. It takes time and attention to notice right and wrong actions and follow up with encouragement and teaching. It takes our time and availability to point out the beauty in the sunset, moon, and stars and to appreciate the One who created them.

The Upside

For the most part, today's parents are more aware of how they are doing their job. There are myriad resources to help us parent effectively. And we are using our past experience to direct us. In the 1950s and 1960s, our parents were limited to Dr. Spock and their parents' examples.

Today, in addition to the plethora of parenting resources available, we have good books and the media to encourage us in our faith walk as well. Because this generation of believers is less inclined to accept pseudoreligion and spirituality, seeking hearts are being satisfied in churches where the worship of Jesus Christ is alive and the grace of God is taught and given. They see true Christianity not only meeting personal needs but having answers for their suffering relationships as well.

Resources are important. Information is powerful. God's wisdom is vital.

The Seven Skills

Our goal with this book is to encourage you to nurture seven emotional skills in your children that will foster intimacy in their relationships. These seven skills provide a foundation to eventually allow our children to worship God, to be intimate with Him, to connect closely with Him, and to enjoy it all.

The seven skills are:

> Respect for authority
> Delayed gratification
> Self-awareness
> Empathy
> Social awareness
> Motivation and persistence
> Hope

Because emotions play such a large part in our attachments to one another and to God, we need to learn to manage them. While emotions can contribute to building connections in relationships, they can also destroy them. Each of the seven skills involves controlling and using emotion to enhance relationships in the home, workplace, neighborhood, and at church. The good news is that these same skills are useful in our relationship with God. What we suggest does not replace your efforts to personally introduce your children to Christ. Nor does it discount the work of the Holy Spirit in calling each of us and making us new creatures in Christ. However, the seven skills are groundwork the Spirit of God can use when He draws our children to the Heavenly Father. Even though we teach them to respect authority, have honorable work habits, relate pleasantly to others, and tell them about who God is, it is only the Holy Spirit who can change their hearts. The true beauty of these seven skills is that they have spiritual implications.

Respect for Authority

Authority figures are everywhere: parents, principals, police, supervisors, elders. Being able to submit to authority figures in our life is necessary for success. Just look at what happens when we don't: joblessness, suspension from school, jail, rebellion in the home and church that separates us from people who love us. Respect for authority starts with the connection made between you and your child. It carries over to other authority figures in your child's life, including God. As God becomes a trusted authority in our lives, we submit to His direction for us and we are blessed by doing what He asks of us. We exercise faith when we submit, believing God is trustworthy. This spirit of cooperation blesses those we work with, and it blesses God tremendously. It reflects a heart attitude and a confidence in an all-knowing Father.

Delayed Gratification

We don't always get what we want. That's just the way life is. The ability to delay our own gratification will decrease the tension that comes when we want something but can't afford it or know that it's not good for us to have. We can train ourselves and our children to put our own desires aside. And we'll be happier for it. This involves managing emotion. God often asks us to wait, so it's important to learn to delay our own gratification. Sometimes God asks us not to participate in something for our own health or well-being. Most of the time obedience reflects self-control, which is a fruit of the Spirit. The way of obedience can be hard, but it is the way to blessing.

Self-Awareness

Possessing self-awareness or having insight is simply being conscious of our own thoughts, feelings, and behaviors. It's powerful because it allows us to share ourselves with others on a deeper level. And it propels us to make necessary changes in our lives. Spiritually, self-awareness benefits us in two ways. Like King David, we are free to be honest with God about our joy and our pain. Also, since we are more aware of our sin, we can experience the freedom of confessing and repenting.

Empathy

Empathy requires being able to accurately sum up what another person may be thinking or feeling based on cues. We can empathize with others when we're able to put aside our own personal distress. But empathy isn't just identifying another's feelings; it includes responding effectively to offer support. More important, empathy helps us understand what Jesus endured to save us.

Social Awareness or Reciprocity

Relationships without reciprocity (give and take) are tiring. Relationships thrive when we expose our thoughts and feelings appropriately as well as listen to those of others. The same is true of our time spent with God. It's dynamic and alive when we share with Him as well as listen for His voice. Our giving back to God in the form of worship, praise, communication, and service happens out of fullness and love for Him rather than a sense of duty. Any other way, it's not sincere reciprocity.

Motivation and Persistence

Successful leaders and employees are motivated and persist through even the dullest tasks. The daily chores of a mother caring for her children require motivation and persistence. Continuing to work at a difficult marriage until it finally turns a corner takes persistence. These twin abilities are the prime movers behind our efforts to know and serve God, especially when He seems silent. God calls us to be disciplined—which is uncomfortable at times. It takes motivation and persistence to seek after God with all of our hearts. Blessings await those who persist and are motivated to know and to serve.

Hope

Finally, having hope sets the tone for our lives. Hope is more than optimism. Hope believes that even in the midst of adverse circumstances, God will prevail. He will give us strength. He will allow good to come from adversity. If we trust God to give us hope and a future, we can look at our children with the same positive expectancy. When we see rebellion or despair, we can hope that God will keep working in all of us until the day of Christ Jesus. Life is no longer a game of chance but an adventure that is without risks (in the eternal sense). Hope builds faith.

A Cord of Three Strands

Eccles. 4:12 says, "A cord of three strands is not quickly broken." As wonderful as the parent-child connection is, it is made complete when it includes Jesus Christ.

At some point in their lives, our children will face challenges. What we have taught up to that point will matter. We know that as our children gradually walk away from us, toward their Heavenly Father, they have a perfect Parent to guide them through whatever they face in life. It makes letting them go easier. And watching them connect with the Father is wonderful indeed.

Introduction Endnotes

1. Bill Ewing, Christian Life Ministries Lay Counseling Class, Level 1, Lesson 3, "Body, Soul, and Spirit," 1999.

2. "50 Activities for Teaching Emotional Intelligence: The Best from Innerchoice Publishing" Level I: Elementary (Torrance, Calif.: Innerchoice Publishing, 1996), 1-15.

3. Nancy Gibbs, "Do Kids Have Too Much Power?" *Time Magazine* (August 6, 2001), No. 31.

1 Respect for Authority

"Correct your son, and he will give you rest; yes, he will give delight to your heart" (Prov. 29:17, AMP.).

As parents, we've heard this verse many times. Some days, in fact, we depend on the assurance it gives us. Am I doing it right? Have I said *no* too much today? Was this really a battle worth fighting with a 2-year-old? With a 17-year-old? Am I building or damaging my child's respect for authority? Good questions. If you've asked yourself questions like these as you raise your children, you're on the right path—you're acknowledging that you're not perfect and that the responsibility of being a parent is great. And if Prov. 22:6—"Train a child in the way he should go, and when he is old he will not turn from it"— strikes you as an awesome task, you're in good company.

What *is* "the way he should go"? Most people will agree it includes a healthy respect for authority. But where does a child acquire *that*? From birth, the relationship a child has with his or her parents will have the greatest impact on that child's dealings with authority figures. But society's impact is relevant too. So before we talk about direct parental involvement, let's get a little perspective on where our culture stands on respect—and disrespect—for authority.

A Bad Rap

What thoughts come to mind when you hear the word *author-ity?* If you've had a good experience with authority figures in your life, the word itself probably doesn't affect you. But if someone has used his or her authority to hurt or manipulate you, chances are the word has negative connotations for you. Today, the word *authority* doesn't give us warm, fuzzy feelings. In fact, it's a repulsive word for much of American society. The perception that authority craves control and stifles the human spirit is, in part, a reaction to misused and abused authority.

The most formative years in my (Pam's) life were in the 1960s and 1970s, when our culture turned a corner. Humanism was the budding philosophy. Protesters rallied with determination for feminism and civil rights and against the Vietnam War. It was a time characterized by anger against authority.

New parents of the 1960s and 1970s decided it was time for a change. Parenting prior to the Vietnam Era was generally *authoritarian.* Discipline was effective in stopping behavior, but many times it was harsh and broke the child's spirit. Effective parenting books were few and far between. And instead of learning from and adjusting the parenting styles used by the previous generation, society swung the pendulum by moving from authoritarian to permissive parenting. This reaction has helped dictate today's lack of respect for and even aversion to *authority.* Baby boomer parents, trying to make up for the way they were raised, have made it their primary goal to be liked. That makes it tough for them to set limits. And it has taken us from the tightly controlled family unit to an almost loosey-goosey one. As a result, we've lost a healthy respect for authority. Do you think you show respect for authority? Take time out to gauge yourself.

Time Out: R-e-s-p-e-c-t

Take this short quiz to measure your R-E-S-P-E-C-T quotient.
- If a cashier forgets to charge you for an item or under-charges you, do you bring it to his or her attention?
- Do you park in a spot reserved for handicapped drivers "just for a second"?

- Do you speed often and only drive the speed limit if a police officer is in sight or you're in a known speed trap?
- Do you tell little white lies to get out of something you don't want to do?
- Do you roll through stop signs if no one else is at the intersection?
- Have you ever skipped buckling your child in a car seat because you didn't have time to transfer it from one car to the other?

If you answered yes to any of these, you're not alone. These are the kinds of things many of us do either because we don't have time to "do it right" or because we've picked up an "I deserve it" attitude. Should your parenting license be revoked if you answered yes to two or more of these questions? No, but you should take a look at your own attitude toward authority. And be honest with yourself: Do you have a healthy respect for "thou shalt not kill" but tend to disregard no parking zones? If you do, chances are your children see your behavior and are learning that it's OK not to follow the rules if you don't like them or if they're inconvenient. It might be time to rethink your own attitude. Write down how you can improve the way you demonstrate respect for those in authority over you. Start small and keep reviewing your list.

What does respect for authority look like in children? Here's a quick list. Put a check in the box next to each item at which you feel your child is adept. If your child doesn't do most of these things, you might want to work on them together. This list is not definitive, but it's a good place to start.

A child who respects authority will:

☐ Address adults appropriately.

☐ Use a respectful tone when talking with others.

☐ Use appropriate eye contact both when speaking and when being spoken to.

☐ Demonstrate a helpful attitude.

Functional Purpose of Authority

Just as games have rules to insure that all players have an equal chance to enjoy them, each system within society has rules for everyone's benefit. According to Kevin Gerald in his book *The Proving Ground,* authority should always have a functional purpose. It serves to prevent chaos, lawlessness, and poor organization. But it's more than preventative. It establishes an environment that allows us to function at an optimal level. For example, if the law didn't protect us from those who steal or murder or drive 100 miles per hour, we would live with significant fear while out in public. If there were no authority structure in school classrooms, no one would learn.

So where did the concept of *authority* come from? From God, who designed it for our freedom and well-being. Notice the paradox? He put authority figures in our lives so we could be all that He created and wants us to be. Let's look at Matt. 28:18-20. Jesus says, "All authority in heaven and on earth has been given to me. Therefore go and make disciples of all nations, baptizing them in the name of the Father and of the Son and of the Holy Spirit, and teaching them to obey everything I have commanded you. And surely I am with you always, to the very end of the age."

Usually when we read this passage, we focus on the command to share the gospel and fail to notice the empowering nature of the first statement. We are equipped to follow this command *because* of Christ's authority in heaven and on earth. He gets underneath us and lifts us up—emotionally and spiritually—to fulfill such a command. He is our coach, our teacher, the lover of our souls. But it is only when we do it His way and under His authority that we are most effective.

The whole idea of authority is hard for many to understand because it's been poorly communicated and even distorted within the Church. Donald E. Sloat, Ph.D., is a psychologist in private practice in Michigan. In his book *The Dangers of Growing Up in a Christian Home,* he writes, "One of the most harmful practices in evangelical homes is parents' use of God and Scripture to control children, avoid personal responsibility, and justify negative child-rearing practices."[1] He suggests that we stay away from using phrases like "Aren't you ashamed of yourself?" and "What do you think Jesus would say if He saw you doing that?" Statements like these and other manipulative, controlling actions give our kids stones and snakes instead of bread and fish (see Matt.

8:7-11). They do more damage to a child's developing concept of God than we realize. Jesus did not abuse His authority by manipulating people into acceptable behavior.

It's important to establish that the role of authority serves a well-founded purpose for the good of the home, workplace, and society. And it bears repeating that in order for any system to function without chaos and turmoil, there must be a leader. But a position of authority requires serious responsibility toward and respect for those under its subjection. That responsibility and respect are the foundation of a healthy relationship.

Using Authority Responsibly

There is no better place to experience healthy relationships than the family. This should be a safe place for children to learn life's most valuable lessons—about loving themselves, others, and God. Granted, the family isn't a perfect place, but ideally, it is a place of grace, where mistakes are made by all. It is safe. When love and respect exist, it's only natural that restitution and reconciliation follow.

We know that kids respond to boundaries. Young children especially thrive when there is an obvious and affirming authority figure. Think of a toddler, we'll call her Annie, who is just figuring out that she's a separate entity from Mom and Dad. How frightening that realization must be! Now picture her in charge of all her own decisions—she can't possibly live up to that responsibility; her brain isn't ready for it yet. She needs someone to tell her—in language she can understand—to hold hands when crossing the street, not to touch the hot stove, and not to put peanut butter in the VCR.

But she also needs balance. As she matures, she needs to learn to make her own decisions—a little at a time and still within the boundaries of safety. So how do you strike that balance? By using a parenting style that teaches your children to respect your authority, one that demonstrates that you fill their lives with structure and order *because* you love them.

Parenting Styles

Styles of parenting are as varied as the people who parent,

but they fall into one of three categories: authoritarian, permissive, and authoritative. The first two styles, authoritarian and permissive, do not nurture emotional intelligence. And both have the potential to produce disrespect for authority and to emotionally shortchange a child. As we've already noted, many permissive parents are the children of authoritarian ones.

An **authoritarian** parent is one who demands obedience to a set standard of conduct. The rules are clear and inflexible. Punishment is often severe on the backside. Parental apologies are few to none. The parent demonstrates a lack of respect for the personhood of the child by behaving with little warmth and responsiveness. And even though the child may outwardly demonstrate respect, inwardly respect doesn't exist because of the bitterness and resentment this type of parenting fosters. This approach tends to produce children with lower self-worth. Children of authoritarian parents are often rebellious or indecisive.

The **permissive** style of parenting, on the other hand, borders on neglect. Structure and boundaries are vague and uncertain. Though the parent is warm and supportive, the child becomes the one in charge. This nonpunitive and affirmative approach places few maturity demands upon the child. The parent demonstrates a lack of respect for the child by not acknowledging the child's need for security through boundaries and limits. The child doesn't respect the parent for abandoning his or her need for discipline and love. As a result, permissive parenting often produces children who are aggressive, have behavior problems, and suffer from low self-worth. These children cry out for structure.

Developmental psychologists tell us that the best outcomes occur when an **authoritative** approach to parenting is taken. Respect for both parent and child can flourish with this approach. Authoritative parents are highly involved. They set limits, explain why limits are set, have high expectations, but are warm and loving. Though these parents exercise firm control at appropriate times, there is a degree of flexibility so their children are not hemmed in with restrictions. The children are eventually given choices, as they are able to assume responsibility for consequences from bad choices. There is a balance between discipline and love. While there are no guarantees that this parenting style produces respectful, well-rounded children, the odds are greatly increased.

We mentioned earlier that God established the concept of authority for our good. The Bible shows us example after example of God's plan for parents as authority figures. Let's take a look at Eli the priest, who chose a permissive approach to parenting his sons.

Eli the Priest

Eli was a judge and high priest of Israel during the time of Samuel, the prophet. He was a good man and delighted in God's service, but he had serious problems parenting his two sons, Hophni and Phinehas. No mention is made of Eli's wife, so we assume he was a single parent who lived in the Temple with his sons. Scripture describes the two sons of Eli as "base and worthless; they did not know or regard the Lord" (1 Sam. 2:12, AMP.).

When people offered sacrifices in the Temple, some of the meat went to the priest and his family. The amount was determined by custom: The sacrifice was put in a pot of boiling water. After a time, a servant (in this case, Hophni or Phinehas) would thrust a fleshhook with three prongs into the water. Whatever amount of meat was brought up on the fleshhook, the priest took for himself. Hophni and Phinehas didn't wait until the meat was fully cooked before bringing it up from the pot. Instead, they poked it while it was still underdone and was less likely to fall off the fleshhook, thereby acquiring more meat for themselves.

Scripture says the Lord considered this sinful act to be "very great" because the sons "despised the offering of the Lord" (v. 17, AMP.). It was personal rebellion against man and God.

Hophni and Phinehas also brought prostitutes into the Temple for their own entertainment—a blatant disrespect for the things of God. Consequently, judgment came to Eli because he knew what his sons were doing and "did not restrain them" (1 Sam. 3:13, AMP.).

Eli's gentle rebuke was not fitting for the rebellion his sons exhibited. His love and kindness to them were mistaken and false. Though he had no power to change their hearts, he could have removed them from service in the Temple. But he chose not to, even after two warnings from God. Eli tolerated his sons' evil.

Clearly, Eli's sons did not respect his authority. Thus, they could not respect God's authority. The window of opportunity to develop this skill had closed for Hophni and Phinehas. Why did Eli choose this passive parenting style that allowed his sons to behave as they did? Not even shame appeared to motivate him to show firmness and tough love. Perhaps it was timidity. We don't know.

But we do know that there's an important lesson for us here: Eli, through omission, demonstrated how important it is to establish an early respect for authority in our children. The outcome for Eli is, in itself, motivation for us. We see firsthand the effects of permissive parenting in Phinehas and Hophni.

Establishing Control

Because of our children's dependence upon us, and their need for structure and security, they naturally look to us to take care of them. They grow to trust us unless we give them reason not to.

You are your children's first teacher. They will naturally look to you for answers and for security. They will sense the authority you have to teach them what they need to know. When they see what they have learned, feel the confidence from learning what you have taught, and the release that comes from personal expression within the boundaries you've given them, they grow to trust your leading. You win a place in their hearts. Your children learn to put themselves under your authority because you have gifted them with security and some personal skills.

We need to clarify the difference between compliance and obedience. An outward respect for authority looks like this: We follow the law; we follow the rules of the company we work for; we follow the commandments; we say and do the things appropriate for the situation and setting we are in. Outside, we look polished and in line to make society, the home, the church, or the work setting function as it should. But does that outward display match what's inside the heart? If we have a genuine desire to obey the law, to follow the rules of the company we work for, to keep the commandments, or whatever—if we do these things because of our devotion to and respect for our authority figures, then we are truly *obedient.* Underneath our desire to obey is emotion—love and devotion for the authority figure.

On the other hand, if we jump through all the right hoops, paste a smile on our faces, but are doing it to avoid consequences or to get a reward, then we are *compliant.* Love and devotion to an authority figure are not part of the motivation. The heart looks different from the outward action. Children start out compliant and learn to be obedient as they grow to trust those in authority over them. Trust in Mom and Dad's love and care is key. When children can trust Mom and Dad to love in spite of misbehavior, they have emotional safety.

As children's relationships with their parents (and other caregivers) develop, their hearts must learn to trust in their parents' goodness. Trust is not built instantly, so we can expect that true obedience in the heart of a child will take a considerable amount of time to develop as well. We can, however, expect a child to *comply,* and that's an important goal during the first five years of life. After a child knows his or her parents can be trusted to meet emotional needs and the child knows how to comply, then true obedience has a chance. Some children are immediately compliant. A strong-willed toddler won't be so willing. Don't wait to start this lesson.

Time Out: Establishing Control

Think carefully about the parenting style your parents used. Did you respect them as authority figures as you were growing up? Were you obedient or merely compliant—or maybe neither? Now examine your own parenting style. Is it the same as or similar to the one your parents used? Are your children obedient or compliant or neither? Do you have the time and energy to be an authoritative parent? Take a moment to reflect on these questions. Write down your thoughts.

Noah

God is all-knowing and all-powerful, and He knows what's best for us. But He does not force His way upon us. His design is that we stay so intimately close to Him that through our fellowship with Him, we can hear what's best. By listening and responding to Him, we come to know and trust that He is all He says He is. Compliance becomes true obedience because we trust Him, even if He asks the ridiculous of us. Such was the case with Noah.

Noah's relationship with God set him apart from everyone else on earth. Scripture says he "was a righteous man, blameless among the people of his time, and he walked with God" (Gen. 6:9). This is significant because he lived in a corrupt society. Scripture says God's heart was filled with pain for what He saw happening on the earth (v. 6, AMP.). But Noah was different. Noah had found favor with God.

God shared His plan with Noah to rid the earth of its violence and depravity, and He assured Noah that his family would be saved if Noah built a big boat in his backyard. God gave Noah explicit instructions for the exact dimensions for the ark and what type of wood to use, right down to the last detail. He told Noah it would save his entire family when the floodwaters came. But Noah didn't know what floodwaters were. He had never even seen rain.

Then God told Noah to bring two of each animal on earth with him and to gather food for the animals as well as for his family. The whole task looked impossible. In fact, it took 100 years to build this huge boat. Can you imagine what the neighbors must have said about him?

Noah and his sons labored over each detail. The animals miraculously came to them, some from far distances. Then one day God told Noah to take his family and the animals into the ark and God would close the door. Noah, typically, obeyed. It was a week before the rains came. It rained so hard the boat began to rise in the water. It rained 40 days and 40 nights. Finally, all Noah and his family could see through the peepholes was water—the earth was covered! And they were the only living creatures left. What an eerie feeling that must have been. And what grief and terror must have been in their hearts for the people who were lost.

Noah's family spent a year caring for one another and the animals in the ark. Imagine the smell and the frustration of caring for some of those loud, unlovely creatures! But Noah did just as God told him. Finally, a dove appeared with an olive branch in its mouth and they knew land must be nearby. They settled on what had been a mountaintop and Noah offered a sacrifice of thanksgiving to God for their safe journey. It was typical of Noah to make his first act one of worship and love for God.

Noah's obedience cost him: He was ridiculed by his friends and neighbors. But he experienced rewards as well: salvation, a fresh start, and intimacy with God. He saw God's hand of protection on him and his family. And he saw how God met his needs on a daily basis. Noah knew what it meant to live out John 15: "Dwell in Me and I will dwell in you . . . I have loved you . . . abide in My love . . . If you keep My commandments, you will abide in My love and live on in it . . . I have told you these things, that My joy and delight may be in you, and that your joy and gladness may be of full measure and complete and overflowing" (AMP.).

Bringing It All Home

How do we become like Noah—obedient to God's authority —and avoid being like Eli who let his children run amuck? There is no single, pat answer, but it has a lot to do with our own attitudes about authority and our own demonstration of respect. The parent-child relationship is not without pain. We are sinful beings —it's as simple as that. But we are also forgiven sons and daughters of a loving Heavenly Father. We will make mistakes. The key is to recognize those mistakes, to "own" them, and to ask for forgiveness—even from our children. This will keep the emotional connection alive between parent and child. It's the persistent parent-child team that will succeed with God's help. Here is one example of a mom who sought help to improve the connection with her child.

Kate

Kate is the mother of two toddlers. She was exasperated because her three-year-old was hitting her. Whenever little Tiffany got mad at her mother, she hit her with both hands. From my

(Pam's) standpoint, Tiffany, at age three, was already mocking her mother. Kate didn't know what to do.

Part of Kate's confusion had to do with her emotions surrounding her own childhood. Her father had spanked her severely in anger. She has decided she doesn't want to spank Tiffany, at least not like she was spanked. Kate was advised in a parenting class to give time outs as a disciplinary measure. But that hadn't been effective for strong-willed Tiffany. This was one of many experiences with Tiffany that eroded Kate's confidence as a parent.

Kate was wise to seek counsel at this stage so she could develop a confidence in herself that would put her back in charge of her toddlers. Counseling and coaching may offer her that, and it's critical that she do this for herself, her children, and her family—right now. What's ahead for Kate will not be easy, but it will be less difficult than enduring more pronounced examples of disrespect as Tiffany gets older. Kate will spend a lot of time and energy, as all parents do who use the authoritative approach. She must become familiar with her child's manipulative tactics, then stay on top of the situation. If she can correct the bad habits with firmness and fairness, she will reap the rich rewards of enjoying the company of her child—and so will others.

It's an investment and a risk to put so much into your parenting. Like the stock market, there are no guarantees for positive outcomes, but there are trends and predictable outcomes if we follow the advice of experts.

Time Out: Who Has Authority?

Is there a child in charge of your home? Based on what you've learned in this chapter, is it possible that you're allowing your child too much authority? Write down what you'll do to shift the authority scales back in your direction.

Does your child avoid making eye contact with those in authority? Pay careful attention to the eye contact you demonstrate for your child. Are you usually cooking or washing dishes while you speak to your child? Make an effort to look your child in the eye when you talk to him or her. Model the kind of eye contact you expect your child to give to others. Get down on your knees or sit on the couch so your faces are on an even level. It's hard to maintain eye contact with someone who is three feet shorter or taller than you. With time, your child's eye contact—and therefore, respect for those to whom he or she speaks—will improve. This is a tough one—it takes time and patience. Stick with it. Other people will enjoy being around your children when they demonstrate a respect for authority. If you think you need some help in this area, see Appendix A for more ideas.

Spiritual Implications

Suppose you work in a company that is large and impersonal and you rarely have a chance to interact with the CEO. You've read the handbook, so you know what the rules of the organization are and what it takes for you to keep your job. But at times you resent demands put on you to produce more for less. You feel as if your family is getting the least of you while the boss you barely know is getting the best part of you. The resentment toward your employer grows and the job becomes less satisfying because a relationship with the person in charge doesn't exist.

Suppose you have not personally experienced the love of God but have heard of the rules God has put in place for all to obey. You know the rules but you don't know the Creator of the rules. Resentment and anger begin to build toward God because of the restrictions you see in this arrangement. And to top it off, He has the power to send you to hell for disobedience. Find any way to warm up to that? No!

The principles that work with earthly parents also work with God, but our human nature gets in the way. If we don't know Him—that is, have an emotional attachment with Him—we turn God into an unwelcome authority figure, an authoritarian parent. We think of Him as a rule-maker and a taskmaster who places demands upon His children and loves them only if they perform correctly. This picture of God is far removed from who He actually is, but it is one way Satan keeps us from respecting God's authority.

It's crucial that we teach our children who God is by talking to them at the same time we parent them with warmth, respect, and firm boundaries. Tell your young children about God's kindness rather than His wrath. Get in the habit of seeing where God has been kind and good to you and your family, then communicate that to your children. Your children will have a better chance of learning to trust in God's love and goodness for them too.

Basic trust that is established early in the parent-child relationship is believed to be the prime precursor to faith in God. David Heller, author of *The Children's God*, believes that continued trust, nurtured through steady and sensitive attention, translates to the emerging of faith in the child.[2] Heller conducted a study of 40 children of four different faiths to depict the perceptions of God in children ages 4 to 12, and what factors influence a child's God-image. He found that the parental imprint is the most frequently occurring family influence on a child's image of God. Both father and mother make contributions, even grandparents. How a parent interprets the role of formal religion for the family, how the parent expresses his or her own particular worldview and ministers to the growth of the child all add to a child's perception. By observing parents, children will deduce if God is someone who is aloof or close to them, what He expects from them, if He is reliable to help them. They will also quickly decide how important they are to God, and if God *wants* to help them.

Leanne Payne, author and counselor, believes something similar to Heller's concept. In her book *Restoring the Christian Soul*, she writes:

> Parents symbolize God to their young. If the Christian father who teaches his son or daughter about God is himself a stern and unfeeling judge, the child will, apart from some very unusual and happy circumstance, perceive God the Father in that way. If a child's Christian parents are impossible to please, the child will almost certainly perceive God in the same way. Until healing takes place . . . such a one cannot hear God's "well done" spoken over him. He cannot understand and receive the affirmation the Father is continually pouring out upon His children![3]

What a responsibility parenting is—but what a privilege as well. We have a responsibility to stay under God's authority so He can lift us up to be the parents we need to be. And we also have the privilege to shape our children's view of God by how we parent. By helping children learn to respect our authority, bringing them beyond compliance to a point of obedience, and by teaching them about the God who loves them, we show them how to respect God's authority. And we give them the chance to discover God's incredible design for humankind.

So be still and listen to God's voice—let Him show you how to be the best authoritative parent you can be. As you do, God will do more than help you. He will allow you to experience intimacy with Him that comes from truly depending upon Him. He will show you His love and mercy so you have more to give your own children.

Time Out: Pray!

As always, bring your concerns to God in prayer. He has promised to listen and to answer. Write down the concerns you will pray about regarding your parenting style, personal attitude about authority, other influences such as television or your children's friends, your ability to control with love and respect, your personal view of God, and teaching your children about God. Lay those concerns at the feet of your Heavenly Father every day.

Chapter 1 Endnotes

1. Donald E. Sloat, *The Dangers of Growing Up in a Christian Home* (Grand Rapids: Mandy Press, 1999), 86.

2. David Heller, *The Children's God* (Chicago: University of Chicago Press, 1986), 142.

3. Leanne Payne, *Restoring the Christian Soul* (Grand Rapids: Baker Books, 1991), 34.

Delayed Gratification

"A person without self-control is as defenseless as a city with broken-down walls" (Prov. 25:28, NLT).

As I (Pam) listened to a popular radio talk show host, one caller found himself in a precarious spot. This married man had received a note from a coworker asking him to meet her after work. She wanted to get to know him better. His question to the radio host was, should he meet with her to tell her he was married or decline? After some rather direct questioning, the host candidly pointed out that the woman probably knew he was married, and her invitation flattered him. The host suggested the caller was entertaining the idea of temporarily feeding his fledgling ego with a woman who didn't care about his fidelity. Yet the man needed advice. He was at a crossroads of going for instant gratification or denying himself for the sake of his marriage. Every day you and I have opportunities to resist temptations that could get us into trouble.

When the alarm went off at 6:00 this morning, I didn't leap out of bed. Oh, how I wanted to stay in the warmth and comfort. Just give me one half-hour more, *please!* Others were counting on me to maintain my morning routine. I resisted the urge to stay in bed. Otherwise, the rest of day would assume a much faster pace. My goal was to avoid that.

I went to the grocery store hungry. Big mistake. The challenge was to resist buying food we didn't need. My goal was to avoid the bigger grocery bill by passing up that shiny bag of chips, mint chocolate chip ice cream, and fresh jumbo shrimp on sale. That hurt.

Then there was the restless lady in a pickup following way too close behind me. I was so annoyed. I wanted to slam on the brakes to get her attention. I imagined her hitting me and getting out of her truck, apologizing. Reason told me it probably wouldn't pan out that way. So I passed on the opportunity. My goal was to keep the car bumper intact and not let this minor annoyance steal my joy.

All day long we are faced with opportunities to resist impulse. It's a key skill for living life to the fullest.

Self-control is at a premium today. Internet pornography beckons us and our kids with enticing advertisements and unsolicited E-mail. Television producers and pop musicians dictate the cultural norms. Drugs, alcohol, tobacco, and sex are available in virtually any high school. Never before have we had access to so much—good and bad—at our fingertips. We need self-control just to survive.

The Marshmallow Challenge

Daniel Golman, in his best-selling book *Emotional Intelligence,* describes a remarkable 1960s study conducted at Stanford University by psychologist Walter Mischel. The "marshmallow challenge" was posed to four-year-olds sitting face-to-face with one delicious marshmallow. The four-year-olds were told that if they waited until the experimenter ran an errand, they could have *two* marshmallows. If they chose to eat one immediately, they could only have that one. The results of the marshmallow challenge exemplify the battle between satisfying our desires for immediate pleasure and temporarily putting aside our own desires for a greater reward.

Some four-year-olds were able to wait what must have seemed an endless 20 minutes for the experimenter to return. To sustain themselves in their struggle, they came up with ways to distract themselves. They covered their eyes, rested their heads on their arms, talked to themselves, sang, played games with their hands and feet, even tried to go to sleep. Because they succeeded in waiting, they were rewarded with an extra marshmallow. About one-third of the children caved in to the pressure and quickly snatched up the lone marshmallow.

When these children became adolescents, they were tracked down to see what their ability or inability to delay gratification as children meant for them as they headed into adulthood. Those who were able to exercise self-control as preschoolers were also doing it as adolescents. Those who were more impulsive as preschoolers were more impulsive as adolescents. The social and emotional results are worth our attention. Golman summarized the results: "The emotional and social difference between the grab-the-marshmallow preschoolers and their gratification-delaying peers was dramatic. Those who had resisted temptation at four were now, as adolescents, more socially competent: personally effective, self-assertive, and better able to cope with the frustrations of life."[1]

On the other hand, the marshmallow grabbers tended to have less social and academic competence. They were more likely "to be stubborn and indecisive; to be easily upset by frustrations; to think of themselves as 'bad' or unworthy; to regress or become immobilized by stress; to be mistrustful and resentful about not 'getting enough'; to be prone to jealousy and envy; to overreact to irritations with a sharp temper, so provoking arguments and fights. And, after all those years, they still were unable to put off gratification."[2]

According to their parents, the group of adolescents with self-control was more academically competent as well. They had considerably higher SAT test scores (a 210-point advantage) than the marshmallow-grabbing group.[3] Golman believes that impulse control contributes more to intellectual potential than IQ. And unlike IQ, impulse control can be learned.[4]

The life skill of being able to delay our own gratification makes a monumental difference whether we are trying to be patient at 3 A.M. with a crying baby or trying to finish medical school. It's the essence of emotional management: keeping our emotions subject to truth and what is best. The goal may be meeting a baby's need to be fed or diapered or becoming a doctor instead of finding an easier, more immediate way to make a living. Every day involves many choices and opportunities to use self-control.

Today, I could have functioned at a much more frenzied pace, suffered from buyer's remorse at the grocery store, filed an accident report with my insurance company, and much more. It's our ability to deny our own immediate gratification that gives us a more optimal daily experience. It buys our freedom.

Time Out: Marshmallow Grabbers

Are you a marshmallow grabber or could you wait 20 minutes so you'd get two marshmallows? What about your children? Would they pass the marshmallow challenge? If you don't know, try a little test at home. If your son is a marshmallow grabber, you know you need to teach him the benefits of delayed gratification. Don't just deny him things he wants. Instead, explain calmly, "I know you want a cookie right now, but we're going to wait until after supper so we'll have room in our stomachs for spaghetti." Acknowledge that you've heard his request and explain why he has to wait. If he still has trouble, continue to acknowledge his feelings. "A cookie really sounds good now, doesn't it? But Mommy said we have to wait until after supper. Can you help me set the table?" Help him deal with his impatience by distracting him with another activity. Later, remind him that since you are finished with dinner, it is a good time to have that cookie he wanted earlier.

The Paradox

Self-control, resisting impulse, delayed gratification are phrases that suggest limits, confinement, restricted fun. Ironically, the opposite is true. The person who has the self-control to deny his or her own immediate gratification for a greater end has *freedom.*

Some of us have learned that the hard way. With freedom comes responsibility. While the call for freedom and doing our own thing sometimes seems like a recent trend, this faulty thinking has been around since Adam and Eve met the serpent in the garden. After the Fall, we became vulnerable to diseases of the body and the mind, to Satan's deception, and to obstacles that keep us from understanding truth. Earth is no longer an eternal beautiful garden but rather a place that will degenerate and perish. How does God maximize His protection of us in this kind of world? He instituted a plan of protection that includes a few dos and don'ts.

Scholars disagree on God's ultimate purpose for the Old Testament Law. Some believe that the rules for "clean and unclean" were established for purposes of good health, and for the handling of meat in Bible times this is undoubtedly true. Whether or not it is still true is debatable. Certainly abstaining from anything questionable is a good idea. Rules such as quarantining individuals with infectious diseases were practiced by the Jews before the general public recognized the need for sepsis controls in hospitals. Other scholars say God only gave different dietary rules to the Jews to keep them from mingling with their pagan neighbors. These rules were suspended in favor of winning the Gentiles, indicating they were never meant to be a law unto themselves (Acts 10).

When Jesus came, the Law was abolished. People no longer needed to trust in symbolic purity. Jesus became the once-and-for-all sacrifice to make us clean.

In the New Testament, God asks us to do several things that seem like Law. But a closer look reveals God is protecting His creation—you and me—from physical, emotional, and spiritual harm. For example, God asks men to have only one wife in 1 Tim. 3:2 and Titus 1:6. He knows that jealousy, feelings of rejection, and anger are predictable among multiple wives of one man. Complete intimacy, as God intended between spouses, is not possible when women are sharing a man.

God tells us in John 10:10 that He wants us to have abundant life. God wants us to be alive inside—physically, emotionally, and spiritually. However, even as God's people, we often miss the point. We end up blaming God for being a taskmaster. We misunderstand the intentions of our Creator, who acts out of goodness and love. Let's look at five areas where self-control brings freedom and protection: food, spending, our words, feelings, and sex.

Food

Oh, the bliss of a really good meal—one where all five senses are overwhelmed. I (Rachel) will never forget the posh New York City restaurant where Jeff proposed to me. Everything about the meal was satisfying to the senses from the sweet aroma of fresh flowers on the table to the soft red velvet tapestries adorning the room to the soothing tones of a string quartet to steak so fine it melted in our mouths. I felt like a princess. At a nod from Jeff, the waiter came over and pulled the table to the side so Jeff could get down on one knee to propose. I was floating on air that night. My senses were completely indulged.

We lived in New York City for a number of years and grew accustomed to the excellent restaurants there. It was easy to over-indulge. Our lives have changed a lot since those years in New York City. Take, for example, a recent fast-food experience. Jeff and the kids were out running errands and decided to pick up supper on the way home. They drove through KFC, where Jeff was tempted to order meals for each of us. Instead, he ordered one meal with two small sides. When he brought it home and put it on the table, my German starch-loving heart was disap-pointed. It looked like so little food. But we all had plenty to eat. Had he brought home what the restaurant advertised as the right amount for two adults and a child, we would have overindulged and stuffed ourselves. It was best for us that Jeff's self-control kicked in at the drive-thru.

Scripture cautions us to avoid overeating and too much wine because the result can be laziness, addiction, poverty, and loss of control (Prov. 23:20-21, 31-35). I've never heard a credible argu-ment against exercising self-control. So why do we struggle with it so much? And how do we teach our children to develop self-control if we struggle with it ourselves?

What and how we encourage our kids to eat can be a good lesson in self-discipline and self-control. We all know about the five food groups, the nutrition pyramid, and how we're *supposed* to eat. But we're bombarded with so many other options that taste better and are more convenient that it's hard to create a menu that's interesting and good for us. And some children are so fussy, they eat separate meals from the rest of the family. I (Pam) knew of one mom who fed her son macaroni and cheese every day for lunch and supper because he refused to eat anything else. This poor boy had an uneducated palate, an under-nourished food intake, and unnecessary fears about food. And he was becoming a slave to his own undisciplined behaviors.

Many of the control battles we fight with our children involve food. It is a smart parent who will not give up in this area and will seek counsel, if necessary, on how to encourage children to *learn* to eat or at least taste what is good for them. They will not only be healthier but also will enjoy the *ability* and the self-confidence to try new foods. They will have disciplined taste buds.

Spending

Mary was an exception to the "poor college student" rule. Her parents' financial situation allowed her access to a lot more spending money than most of her peers. In fact, I (Pam) felt frumpy next to her.

Mary went home for the weekend in the fall of our freshman year to look for a dress for a fraternity banquet. She found a beautiful dress—and a pair of cords, a new sweater, a new down ski coat, and a new suit. I remember thinking, *How can anyone afford to spend that much money in one weekend?*

After college, Mary married Greg, who was financially conservative. Love melded these two hearts together, but they couldn't have been further apart in the ways they approached money. Greg wanted to save enough for a sizeable down payment on a house, so they lived on a budget for several years. Mary's spending habits were at the heart of many arguments. By the time their children came along, Mary was tired of sacrificing the finer things in life for their long-term goals. She longed for the days when she just drove to the mall and spent whatever amount it took to make her feel and look better. It was a battle to push the desires aside and not blame Greg for denying her the pleasures she had indulged in for her first 23 years.

Mary had two choices. She could grow increasingly bitter toward her husband or she could learn to see things for what they were. Either way, it was a harder road *because* she hadn't learned to control her spending at an early age. Mary's attitude of entitlement made her marriage more difficult. She struggled, not knowing how to cope without spending.

How can we teach our children self-control when it comes to money? Taking our children to the mall and occasionally walking out with nothing is a simple but huge lesson. They will learn that it's quite possible to go into a store without buying anything.

In America today, the average family's credit card debt is more than $9,000. Add a monthly interest rate of about 15 percent to the bill, and it's no wonder many people can't get out of debt. The momentary pleasure in acquiring the stuff on the bill is costing the consumer a huge price in the end. Imagine the defeat the consumer who overcharges each month must feel. But imagine the victory this same consumer will feel as he or she exercises discipline to steadily climb out of this bondage. That's what it is—financial bondage. Once we taste freedom, we gain confidence, knowing we never want to go back to being trapped by debt. It's the reward of self-control and delayed gratification. Advertisers have convinced us that we can afford anything on a payment plan. But the rule of thumb—*don't buy it if you don't have the cash for it*—is a good one to apply to most situations. Of course, most of us wouldn't have cars or homes if we used that rule for everything. We need to be smart about what debts we can handle and exercise firm self-control on the others.

There are several resources to help us teach children as early as preschool age to manage money wisely. (See Appendix B.) If you struggle yourself in this area, get help from a financial or consumer credit counselor. By getting help for yourself, you will give your children a gift as well. You will buy your family freedom from the guilt of overspending and the constant worry of not having enough to pay the bills.

Words

If there is one test of discipline that outshines them all, it's how we use our mouths. It feels good to satisfy our frustration, our fears, our need for attention with sensational, sometimes thoughtless and untimely words. I (Pam) speak from practical experience. The best way to teach our children control over the words they use is to model it ourselves. Model by apologizing for misspoken, harsh, disrespectful words to others. Say, "I'm sorry I yelled at you." "I'm sorry I talked about that store clerk like that. I was frustrated and that was the wrong way to show it." Then teach your children how to edify others with their words. "I really like your teacher, Hannah. It's obvious she likes her class. Will you tell her I said that?" A large part of the teaching rests on how we as parents speak to our children and what we put up with. Take the following example.

Sophie's mother made an innocent mistake and 16-year-old Sophie verbally berated her mother in front of her friends. Her mom excused herself to the bedroom and sobbed. Unfortunately, Sophie had never been confronted about her verbal outbursts. No one told her they were unacceptable and hurtful. She should have learned about the consequences for this kind of behavior years earlier. Instead, Sophie loses because she didn't learn to get her point across in a more respectful manner. Her mother loses because Sophie's verbal assaults are hurtful and embarrassing. Sophie's friends lose because they feel uncomfortable and confused. There are no winners.

In their book *Encouragement*, Dr. Larry Crabb and Dr. Dan Allender say, "[Words] are much like a sharp knife that in the hands of a surgeon can heal, but in the hands of a careless child can kill."[5] It's our goal as parents to teach our children to be surgeons with their words. But that's not always easy. I (Rachel) have been blessed with a parrot for a daughter. At three, Calista imitates not only what I say but how I say it. Some days, it's like fingernails on a chalkboard and I realize I need an attitude adjustment when I hear her using an unpleasant tone of voice. But surprise, surprise. When I speak politely in a pleasant tone, she does too. Do your children a favor and teach them how to express themselves appropriately. They will enjoy the freedom of closer relationships and never regretting their own words if they are taught to choose their words wisely.

Anger

Would you choose to live with a rattlesnake in your house? That's what we do when we cling to anger. God never said anger was bad. He just said to take care of it before the end of the day. That way we get the snake out of the house and reduce the chance of being bitten by it.

Snakebites aside, there are actual health benefits of dealing with anger appropriately. Research has shown a link between hostility and heart disease. Those of us who don't know how to express anger appropriately are at greatest risk. In his book *Stress and Your Child*, Archibald Hart describes how the whole body prepares to defend itself when we become angry.

> The brain releases both hormonal and neuronal messengers. The eyes, the facial muscles and heart, stomach, spleen, bowel and bladder all get signals and go into special emergency mode. Blood vessels of the skin contract, sweat is released on the hands and feet, blood pressure goes up, blood sugar is released, the cholesterol level rises, adrenaline surges and the brain goes into high gear. When the anger passes, then one experiences its aftermath as the body system returns to normal. These can include headaches, stomach pains, diarrhea and exhaustion . . . If prolonged, however, this emergency response increases wear and tear in many of our systems and eventually causes permanent damage.[6]

Anger can become dangerous if we don't know how to act on it. In such cases, we use our anger to manipulate others, release frustration, and to hold others at arm's length. Contrary to previous thought, venting or free expression of anger often reinforces and perpetuates the energy behind it. But our children can avoid these negatives if we teach them to respond appropriately to their own anger when they are young.

Begin by telling your child the truth—that *feeling* angry is not a sin but a signal or an alarm he or she should pay attention to. Something is wrong. When the smoke alarm goes off in your house, you turn attention to what is burning. The same is true for anger. Young children might need help associating their feelings and behavior with the word.

Most of the time it's our immediate reaction when we're angry that gets us into trouble. Here's where the concept of "time out" can be helpful. When anger erupts, a cooling down period is essential to allow the body to reset itself so one can think more objectively. I (Rachel) have been known to give myself a time out when Calista's three-year-old antics are getting the better of me. We get a few minutes away from each other, we each cool down, and then we can discuss the situation more rationally. Time outs used too often may become ineffective, so try not to use them for every small infraction.

Once Calista and I have both cooled down, I try to help her figure out what just happened. I talk to her and help her explore what made her so mad. Many times talking about it rationally can have a soothing effect on the body. Were her feelings hurt? Was she afraid of something? Did she not get her way? She needs to problem solve with me. And this may be an opportunity to clear up a misunderstanding or teach her about better ways to express anger.

Anger is meant to be temporary. If we can help children get in the habit of letting go of anger, we have given them a skill that will make them healthier. A few days after Calista had seen the Veggie-Tales video "LarryBoy and the Angry Eyebrows," she told me (Rachel), "Mommy, my eyebrows are angry." It took me a minute to put it together, but then we were able to talk calmly about what had made her mad. Then she said, "Bob [the Tomato] says God wants us to let go of our anger." God bless Phil Vischer and Big Idea for helping me teach my daughter a tough concept.

Time Out: Dealing with Anger

Talk to your children about letting go of anger, then model it for them. The next time you are angry, tell them what behavior upset you, tell them you need a few minutes to calm down, then discuss the situation rationally. You may even tell your children, "I'm done being angry now, but let's talk about our no-hitting rule."

Abraham's Wife, Sarah

Anger also can be a mask for fear. Our fears are so powerful at times that the thinking brain finds it nearly impossible to reason with the fearful emotion. In Sarah's case, her fear of not having a child in her old age led her to take matters into her own hands. She paid a dear price for not being able to wait.

God gave Sarah a big assignment. He gave her a strong-willed personality, then asked her to delay having children in a culture and time when barrenness was considered a disgrace. Sarah probably pleaded with God for decades about her infertility.

God had already told Abraham his descendants would be as numerous as the stars. No doubt Abraham shared this news with his wife. In her desperation, she finally suggested he take her handmaiden, Hagar, to produce a child.

The emotional price she paid was enormous. Jealousy, bitterness, and strife dogged Sarah's footsteps and those of Hagar as a result of that decision. In Sarah's case, her need to give Abraham a child was greater than her ability to wait on God's perfect timing. She doubted God would come through for her and Abraham. She was well beyond childbearing years, and God hadn't given her a child. So Sarah decided she would handle the situation herself.

Sarah got what she wanted. But she and Hagar soon came to hate each other. This affected Sarah's relationship with Abraham, whom she blamed. She had animosity toward Ishmael, Hagar's son, who, in turn, resented Sarah's son Isaac when he was born according to God's plan. Sound like a soap opera yet?

To have peace in his household, Abraham sent Hagar and Ishmael away. And Sarah had to witness Abraham's pain over losing his firstborn son.

To this day, the descendants of these two sons are at odds. Ishmael's descendants are Arabs and Isaac's descendants are Jews. Their legacy of pain and warfare continues in today's Middle East. Sarah couldn't wait, and it has cost generations down through the centuries.

Sex

Never has the world been bombarded with sexuality the way it is today. In the heyday of *I Love Lucy*, Lucy wasn't allowed to say the word *pregnant* on TV. Now ads for Viagra are commonplace, and nearly nude models sell us underwear and shampoo. America has a preoccupation with sex. It's on the airwaves 24/7, and our children are watching and listening. It does little good to try to shelter them completely from the Internet or TV. The better solution is to give them the ability to delay their own gratification.

Randy and I (Pam) followed Josh McDowell's advice for dating when it came time to let our teenage girls date. They asked, "When can I date?" We responded, "That depends." It depended on their ability to say *no* to sexual pressure. We spent a fair amount of time talking openly with them about God's design versus what our culture conveys. We discussed the physical, emotional, and spiritual hurt and consequences of giving yourself to someone other than your husband. It was field training before the game. The real test would come on dates. And everyone gets the test! When we were convinced they had strong convictions about sexual purity, they could go. We hoped their emotions would be made subject to their convictions.

God gave us boundaries so sex would remain a gift. He knew the consequences for us when it happens outside of marriage. But because it's a powerful drive that can temporarily satisfy a deep longing to be close to another person, we are all vulnerable. What makes us strong is an ability to delay our gratification when we're presented the opportunity. Our thinking brain reminds us that it is in our best interest to follow God's plan and avoid life-threatening diseases, unplanned pregnancies that will alter our lives forever, and emotional hurt and shame.

How do you get your kids to that point? One way is to talk openly and honestly with them. Answer their questions without making them feel dirty or ashamed for asking. Give them opportunities to delay gratification in other areas of their lives. Once you've mastered that skill in other areas, it's much easier to apply it to sexual desires.

Fostering the Ability to Delay Gratification

How you train your children from the beginning has a lot to do with how well they will be able to delay gratification. Here are some practical ways you can establish good habits in your children.

Resist the urge to buy your children whatever they want. Help them learn to appreciate the value of what they buy by giving them an allowance with the option to earn more by doing extra jobs. When it's age appropriate, let them use this money to purchase their own toys and clothing. They will benefit from the experience of waiting until they save enough money for what they want.

The need for instant gratification goes hand-in-hand with an attitude of entitlement. Establish good work habits in your children to minimize feelings of entitlement. That doesn't mean you should treat them like indentured servants. But if children are not asked to make a contribution to the household by doing various jobs, they will lack confidence in their own abilities and worth. And they will drive you crazy. A good work ethic combats laziness and promotes self-control and self-discipline. Start young. A two-year-old can help put his or her toys away. A three-year-old can help empty the dishwasher. A four-year-old can help fold laundry and put it away. You get the picture. Avoid connecting regular chores and allowance. Each person does chores to serve the family as a whole, not to earn money. Save any connection between chores and money for special one-time or infrequent tasks.

Minimize your children's television intake. Give them a certain number of television viewing hours per week that they can "buy" with your discretion. Most television—even children's programming—encourages disrespectful language and entitled attitudes. Research shows that the mere act of watching television makes a child's brain go on autopilot. They have better things to do with their time.

Insist that your children finish their homework before being allowed to watch television, play video games, or pursue other leisure activities. Academic success often depends upon hard work and putting aside our own desires in order to achieve. Reward your children for their diligence more than their successes.

Spiritual Implications

How is the ability to delay gratification going to impact a child's eventual intimacy with Christ? The three key ways it will make a difference are **obedience, avoiding heartache,** and **being prepared for Kingdom work.**

First, obedience is pretty hard if you think God is asking you to do one thing and you prefer to do another. But if you've had some practice making your emotions subject to what is right or needed, obeying God is easier. Obedience may mean giving up something you treasure such as time, money, or material things in order to show someone your love. It may mean persisting at a dull task until God leads you elsewhere. Or it could be as simple as turning the TV off to have a conversation with your spouse. A necessary element of obedience often is giving up your own agenda for a greater good that will bring freedom and delight in the end.

God always has your freedom in mind. "It is for freedom that Christ has set us free. Stand firm, then, and do not let yourselves be burdened again by a yoke of slavery" (Gal. 5:1). Freedom is found in the security and confines of God's personal plan for you and your children and maintained by a disciplined lifestyle. It often requires putting off satisfying your immediate wants. There's that paradox again! But discipline isn't so hard when it's a habit.

Second, God wants you to have _inner strength_ to avoid heartache. Sometimes God asks you to deny yourselves opportunities or things that would bring instant or temporary gratification that in the long run would be harmful for you. And sometimes God asks you simply to wait for Him. If you are especially anxious about your own agenda, it's tempting to "help God along" to minimize your own distress, like Sarah did.

The art of delaying gratification provides inner strength that will help you wait. It will enable your child to be a faithful spouse when tempted. It will give you stamina and patience with a crying baby in the middle of the night.

Third, you are better prepared to go where God leads when you have the capacity to put your own agenda aside. What if God asks your adult child to go to a foreign land without all the comforts of home to tell others about Jesus? Will your child allow the status quo to overshadow the will of God because he or she is unaccustomed to inconvenience? Or will your child be equipped to say, "Here I am, Lord. Send me," because he or she knows what it is to deny oneself for a greater end. Of course, there are many factors that play into a decision like this, but a big one is the ability to deny the need for instant gratification.

Self-control, self-discipline, and delaying immediate gratification is a lifelong process that begins in childhood. You will shape your child's approach to life by modeling and teaching this art. It will be a basis for obedience and service in God's kingdom.

Chapter 2 Endnotes

1. Daniel Golman, *Emotional Intelligence* (New York: Bantam, 1995), 81.

2. Ibid., 82.

3. Ibid., 193.

4. Ibid., 83.

5. Larry Crabb and Dan Allender, *Encouragement* (Grand Rapids: Zondervan, 1984), 22-23.

6. Archibald Hart, *Stress and Your Child* (Dallas: Word, 1994), 212.

3 Self-Awareness

"Behold, you desire truth in the inner being; make me therefore to know wisdom in my inmost heart" (Ps. 51:6, AMP.).

Jack is a talkative and perceptive four-year-old. One night, his mother, Sherry, sat beside his bed to tuck him in and to pray. She prayed that Jack would grow closer to Jesus. But afterward, she noticed Jack's lip quivering.

"Jack, what's wrong?" she asked.

He replied, "I don't want to get to know Jesus better. He took Grandpa and won't bring him back."

Jack was angry with God and figured if he knew Jesus better, then Jesus would take him somewhere away from the security of his mom and dad. Jack was beginning to make sense of his grandpa's recent death and to articulate some of his feelings about it. His concept of Jesus, at that point, was as a death courier for God. Jack wanted no part of it.

Certainly, it was a good thing that he was able to talk about his fear so his mom could dispel his developing misconceptions about God. Even Jack's limited self-awareness brought him some comfort as he was able to express his fears to his mom.

The Value of Self-Awareness

Very simply, self-awareness is paying attention to what we feel or think. We have a conscious awareness of what is going on inside us. This includes what we value, our strengths and weaknesses, attitudes, habits, and even some insight into motives.

Those who have emotional maturity or emotional competence are proficient in handling their emotions. They have the ability to bring their emotions under control. Self-awareness is a precursor to that ability. Those with self-awareness recover from bad moods easier and are able to more authentically communicate who they really are to other people. Their inside feelings and thoughts match their outside expressions. They have the ability to understand what others feel like in similar circumstances.

More Control over Self

Self-awareness gives us more control over our feelings and actions. God made our brains to work like a partnership—the emotional brain (limbic system) and the thinking or rational brain (neocortex) work together and support each other to make our life experiences more satisfying.

For example, you are standing on the cliffs overlooking the Maui coastline in Hawaii. Your eyes take in the beautiful blue water. You drink in the sunshine, marvel at how the water splashes against the rocks. Your heart is glad and you know it. Your emotions allow you to take pleasure in the scenery and feel gratitude for it. Your rational mind protects you from jumping because you know you'll get hurt. Both emotion and rationality make it an optimal experience. One without the other would make the experience dull, unappreciated, even life-threatening.

The emotional part of our brain is like a surveillance camera located in the amygdala, a storehouse for all of our emotional memories. These emotional memories might be the fear we felt when a tornado threatened our lives, the sadness and insecurity when we were left out of school activities, the delight from eating a fresh baked apple pie with ice cream. The emotions are the first to experience an event, and they are the first to react.

If an intruder enters our house, our first reaction of fear or surprise comes from the amygdala. Immediately it sends a message for the body to release adrenaline so we're ready to fight or flee. Then the emotional brain starts communicating with the thinking brain, which uses its information and wisdom to control the fear from the emotional brain. Its rational quality helps balance the fear with a sensible plan for the situation at hand. Proceed with caution, stay out of sight, take something to protect yourself, don't strike too soon, this may be someone you know—all rational thoughts from the neocortex.

Without heightened emotion, we may not move fast enough to save ourselves. Without rational thought, we may end up killing someone. Ideally, both parts of the brain work together. However, the emotional brain can—and often does—overreact. We can be consumed by our emotions, the emotional brain can refuse to listen to or fail to hear the thinking brain, or the thinking brain can base its rationality on lies.

But if we have a conscious awareness of how we feel, the thinking brain has a better chance of talking sense into our emotional reactions. Thus, we respond with more control.

Time Out: What Rules—Emotion or Reason?

Are you more emotional or rational in handling unexpected situations? With time, are you able to let truth and reason work with emotions such as excitement, fear, and despair? Think through your reaction the last time you were afraid. With practice, you can create a balance between emotion and reason. It takes some work if you're wired to react with 90 percent emotion. I (Rachel) tend toward the paranoid. I've had to teach myself to think more rationally when I'm struck with fear. Instead of a panic-stricken *What's that noise?* I try to think through the situation. *The doors are locked. The alarm is on. It sounded like a book fell off a shelf.* I calm myself down and then go investigate.

Children are often irrational when they're afraid of something. Many nights, Calista says, "Nothing's coming to my room, right?" when we put her to bed. We assure her that Jesus is always with her and that Mommy and Daddy are just down the hall.

Pay attention to your reaction to unexpected situations or fears and, if you don't have it already, work toward a balance between emotion and reason. Then you can help your children achieve this balance as well.

Connection with Others

Another benefit of having self-awareness is using it to connect with others and find comfort, as in Jack's case. Jack knew what he *didn't* want—to be associated with the Jesus he thought he knew. To a degree, he was aware of feeling mad and afraid. If he hadn't communicated this to his mom, he would have maintained his erroneous beliefs about God. Since he was able to express himself, he found comfort from a tender and insightful moment with his mother.

Many children can't afford to feel. Life's circumstances are too painful and it's just easier to tuck the sadness and anger away somewhere. Perhaps they haven't been given permission to feel. In families where truth is risky—including Christian families where pressure to look good is fierce—an unspoken rule is "don't feel." Each member in the family is obligated to abide by that rule in order to maintain pseudopeace in the family. This learned way of coping with life makes feelings difficult to access. Relationships within this type of family are not honest, intimate, or affirming. Twelve-year-old Megan knows this firsthand.

Megan's parents were divorcing. She was unemotional and nothing seemed to move her. She was the oldest of three children and her role in the family was to be caregiver for her younger sisters. Her parents had been in their own pain for years, so it was inconvenient for the children to have permission to feel.

Megan's way of coping allowed her to manage her responsibilities and get through her painful circumstances, but she was emotionally detached from others. Her friendships were superficial at best because she couldn't share a piece of herself with friends. There was much about herself even she didn't know. Her feelings were tucked away, hidden.

The deeper levels of communication involve sharing feelings and thoughts. That's where intimacy is found. If we're unaware of how we feel and think, it's impossible to share ourselves with others. We miss out on intimacy.

Time Out: Emotional Checkup

Think about recent conversations you've had with your

friends or your spouse. Were you able to move beyond the weather and kids' schedules to share what you are *really* thinking and feeling? If not, try it. Start with a safe topic and ask questions like "What do you think about . . . ?" "How do you feel about . . . ?" Then share what you think and feel too.

Understanding for Others

A third benefit to having self-awareness is gaining understanding of how others feel. As they say, it takes one to know one. If your child knows what it feels like to be rejected on the playground, he or she is more apt to have compassion for another child experiencing the same thing. Chances are, your child will offer the hurt child some comfort.

When my (Pam's) son, Michael, was born, my friend Susan was in the same hospital. Her first child had been born two days before Michael. She stopped in my room to say good-bye as she was leaving the hospital. She was less talkative than usual and seemed preoccupied. I knew almost instantly what was happening inside her, because I had the same feelings beginning about three days postpartum with my first two children. She had the blues, and I could empathize with her immediately. She was yearning for someone to talk with and pray with, someone who could be a resource and encourage her as a new mom. I knew how desperately she needed that. I also knew I could help because of my own experience with postpartum depression.

Reading the visible evidences of feelings in others is easier if we've been there. We have a better idea of how to help others because we know what helped us or would have helped us in a similar situation.

Time Out: Being an Emotions Coach

Self-awareness is an important building block to emotional health. Spend time this week being your children's "emotions coach." You can begin to teach your children self-awareness by helping them identify their feelings *(That puzzle frustrates you, doesn't it?)*; who they are as persons *(You're such a good reader!)*; and how God feels about them *(God thinks you're pretty cool!)*.

Every day, tell your children how you feel about them. Remember, you don't always have to say a pat "I love you." Be creative and spontaneous!

Teaching Self-Awareness to Children

Label Emotions

Four-year-old Molly slammed her two-year-old brother Matt's finger in the door accidentally. There was blood, panic, and a phone call to the emergency room. Molly stood by, watching and feeling terribly guilty. She said out loud, "I want to go with my brother. It was my fault." She didn't say how she felt, but her mom knew by her reaction and the circumstances that she was worried and probably felt remorse.

After it was all over, Molly's mother taught her about being careful and how to associate her feelings with *sad, scared,* and *sorry.* She said, "That made you sad and scared when Matt got his finger caught in the door, didn't it? Even though you didn't mean to hurt him, he still got hurt. The door is too heavy to slam. I bet you're sorry that happened." If Molly didn't have those two words *sad* and *sorry* in her vocabulary before, she does now. She knows what feelings go with those words.

You are your children's emotions coach. Help them collect feeling words by identifying them when you see them. We want to teach our children to label the emotions they feel and associate them with what goes on in the body. "Bobby, you look mad right now. What's going on?" "Sarah, what made you so happy just now?" For a while when she was two and a half, my (Rachel's) daughter would show her anger by hitting things like the couch or the table or by making loud, unattractive noises. I realized that she didn't have a clue what she was feeling or how to tell me about it. All I had to do was talk to her about it and help her identify her feelings: "Cali, are you mad because Mommy told you to stop playing? You were having fun playing and you don't really want to run errands, right?" A puzzled look from Cali, as if to say, *How did you know?* Then, "Yes." "Honey, all you have to do is say, 'Mommy, I'm mad because I want to stay and play and you told me to stop and get in the van.' Then Mommy can tell you what we have to do and when we'll be able to come back to play." It also helped that she loved Mercer Mayer's Little Critter books and we had been reading *I Was So Mad*. The book helped her identify with Critter's feelings, label them, and make the connection to her own feelings. The beautiful thing about labeling what we feel is that it helps us express our feelings.

Dr. John Gottman, author of *Raising an Emotionally Intelligent Child*, believes that being able to express our emotion with words has a soothing effect on the body, soul, and spirit. *Talking* about how we feel helps us make sense of our experiences. Children who are able to soothe themselves in this manner are more likely to concentrate better, have better peer relationships, higher academic achievement, and good health.[1]

Introduce feeling words into your child's vocabulary, explaining what they mean with other words or sitting down with them and drawing facial expressions. Teach your child how to use "I" statements by using them yourself. ("I felt ____ when ____ happened.") My (Rachel's) friend Sharon learned this the hard way with her children. She was raised in a strict, authoritarian household and her father's way of communicating was to demean her ("You're such a brat") or to make empty threats ("If you don't stop that right now, I'll stop the car"). Without realizing it, she used the same methods with her kids. But the demeaning comments just fueled the bad behavior. *Tell me I'm a brat and I'll act even more like one.* And the kids caught on quickly that Mom's threats meant nothing. If you can't or won't follow through on a threat, it's no good and kids know it. One day, Sharon heard another mother in a store tell her rambunctious children, "If you don't stop that this instant, we will leave this store." What's wrong with that? First, it was being in the store that the kids were balking at. A threat to leave the store *because* of their bad behavior would only enhance it. Second, the mother had a cart full of items she intended to purchase, and she was standing in the checkout line. She had no intention of leaving the store after she'd spent all that time filling her cart.

Something clicked for Sharon, and she saw herself. When we talked about it, she asked me to help hold her accountable while she worked to change her behavior. She knew it would take her a while to record over those old tapes running through her head. Now she works hard to use "I" statements such as, "I am getting angry because you are bouncing balls in the aisle and I asked you not to. Please come stand by me until I'm ready to go." She's also becoming a master of distraction. She's learned that kids often act their worst when they're bored or tired. So when she senses that happening, she can now make up a game on the spot or ask for some help: "Mark, we need three cans of tuna. It's at the end of the aisle. See how quickly you can get them and bring them back to the cart." Kids love to be useful. Or "Tina, I see three orange boxes on this shelf. Can you find any blue ones?"

Time Out: Using Feeling Words

Below is a list of feeling words. You've probably felt each of these at least once. Chances are, your kids have—or will—too. Help them label their feelings. With preschoolers, use more general terms such as *angry, happy, sad, afraid.* As kids get older, identify the more specific and complex feelings listed here. Make your own list of feeling words with your kids. Use this list to get started.

Accepted, affectionate, afraid, alarmed, annoyed, anxious, appreciated, awkward, bad, beautiful, betrayed, bitter, bold, bored, brave, burdened, comfortable, confident, cowardly, creative, curious, deceitful, delighted, depressed, deprived, desperate, determined, different, disappointed, distracted, eager, embarrassed, empty, envious, exhausted, foolish, free, friendly, frustrated, glad, grateful, guilty, gullible, happy, helpful, helpless, homesick, honored, hopeful, hopeless, hostile, hurt, ignored, impatient, inadequate, incompetent, independent, inferior, inspired, isolated, jealous, joyous, judgmental, jumpy, lazy, lonely, lovable, loving, loyal, miserable, misunderstood, nervous, nice, optimistic, outraged, overwhelmed, panicked, peaceful, persecuted, pleased, possessive, preoccupied, pressured, quiet, refreshed, rejected, relaxed, relieved, remorseful, restless, sad, satisfied, shocked, shy, silly, sorry, stunned, tempted, tense, threatened, tired, touchy, trapped, unappreciated, uneasy, uptight, used, vulnerable, wonderful, worried.

Truthful Insight

Because of your platform to influence, you will be your children's primary teacher of what is true in their world and what is true about themselves. Your affirmation of their strengths and challenge of their weaknesses will tell them about who they are. Their perception of who God is also can depend a great deal on what they learn from you about God. Of course, outside influences will inform it too—teachers, church leaders, coaches, friends, and so forth. But if you have a solid relationship with your children, you will probably be their greatest influence. The rationale they use in their thinking brains to monitor their emotional brains is based on what they know to be true.

Try to avoid putting all your children into the same category, expecting that one should respond and behave like another or like you do. This means studying each child to learn his or her temperament style. We all have unique temperaments creatively given by God. Unlike our personalities, our temperaments are not influenced by environment.

Knowing your children's temperament types or blends will help you affirm who they are. Mother and daughter Florence and Marita Littauer have written a book called *Personality Plus for Parents* about four God-given temperament styles: melancholy, sanguine, choleric, and phlegmatic. Each temperament style determines how we react to people, places, and things, how we interact with our environment, and how we perceive ourselves and the people who love us. When we have some insight into how God made us and our child—apart from environmental influence—we can accept and understand our God-given strengths as well as where we are vulnerable with weakness. We'll also have more information and insight to parent our children as individuals.

Dr. Gary Smalley and Dr. John Trent also have a "personality inventory" in their program, *Homes of Honor*. They use animals to describe the four major temperament types: lion, beaver, otter, and golden retriever. This program has proved immensely helpful for my (Rachel's) sister-in-law, Jan, and her family. Jan uses each child's temperament type to figure out why they respond to situations the way they do. One day, seven-year-old Aaron was playing with two-year-old Calista, who wanted to walk on Aunt Jan's treadmill. Aaron didn't realize Calista had never been on a treadmill and didn't know the floor would move under her, so he turned it on. Calista fell and began to wail. As soon as Mommy arrived, Aaron ran to his room and cried. He was mortified that he had done something to hurt Calista. Cali got over the incident long before Aaron did. Jan knew her son's temperament well enough to know it would not help at all to force him to apologize to his cousin—he already had more remorse than necessary. First, she needed to help him realize that Calista was OK and that it had been an accident.

The danger, of course, of any such system for identifying temperament types is to put a person in a box. Dr. Smalley and Dr. Trent remind readers that everyone has one *dominant* temperament type that is informed by varying levels of each of the other types as well. So be careful not to overlabel your children. Use the system to give you more insight into your child's personality type, but remember that each individual is wonderfully unique —by God's design. See Appendix C for more information about temperament and personality resources.

Time Out: Temperament Types

Look at *Personality Plus for Parents* or *Homes of Honor* or a similar program. Find out what temperament type each member of your family has. Talk about how your tendencies affect the way you react to different situations.

It's important to learn to let truth dominate the thinking part of our brains. It's truth that sets us free, just as Jack was relieved when he learned that Jesus was not a death courier. When we line up our experience with the truth, we are in a much better position to make good decisions and to problem-solve. This is exactly what we need to begin to teach our children to do as soon as they can reason—usually around age three.

Beginning when our children are young, we need to be perceptive enough to see their confusion based upon what they tell us, what the circumstances are, or by their behavior. Sherry was able to comfort and correct some of Jack's faulty logic about death, heaven, and Jesus just by asking some questions and talking with him. She spoke the truth as she knew it on these subjects and held it up against Jack's beliefs in a way that minimized his fearful thoughts so they didn't have so much power. It was the beginning of helping Jack change his mind about a lie he believed.

Here's an example of a mom who helps her 11-year-old son see the truth as she picks him up from school:

Mom: Hi, Kevin. How was your day at school?

Kevin: Not very good.

Mom: Why's that?

Kevin: Well, all the kids were teasing me about the funny way I say my s's since I got my braces on.

Mom: I bet that didn't make you feel too good.

Kevin: Yeah, Nathan just wouldn't stop. He kept laughing at me and saying how funny it sounded.

Mom: How about Ian? Did he tease you too?

Kevin: No, but Laura did. She and Nathan were the only ones.

Mom: Oh, so it was just those two, and not everyone?

Kevin: Yeah, I just wish I didn't have to have these braces. They hurt so bad and they make me look stupid!

Mom: What do you think they'll feel like in a week, say, next Monday? *(Addressing the pain problem first, she tries to get him to think of how the pain will soon end.)*

Kevin: The dentist said it should get better after a few days, so it might get better.

Mom: Who said you looked stupid? *(Addressing the second issue)*

Kevin: No one, I just do!

Mom: Boy, it's a good thing you had clear braces put on, and not silver ones, or they'd be more noticeable.

Kevin: Yeah, I guess.

For most of us, the battles with negative thoughts about ourselves and how others perceive us happen daily. We have an enemy who seeks to destroy us, who goes after our thoughts with reckless abandon, frequently convincing us of our inadequacies by telling us what bad parents we are, how old and unattractive we're becoming, and how worthless we are. If you are a believer in Christ, you need to know who you are in Christ. The misrepresentations Satan feeds us need to be lined up against what God says about us. Compare the two—routinely—and extinguish those fiery darts thrown your way.

It's important to note that we're not equating self-awareness with self-esteem. Self-esteem puts a premium on feeling good about self, making self the focus. Unlike self-esteem, a Christian's perspective of self-awareness encompasses God's involvement in creating us and His destiny for us, personally. It's exciting, hopeful, and affirming of who we are as individuals. We can use it to make connections with others and with God.

To learn more about what the Bible has to say about who we are and how God feels about us, look at Dr. Neil Anderson's "Who I Am in Christ," from his book *Victory Over the Darkness*. Dr. Anderson is founder and president of Freedom in Christ Ministries. To read "Who I Am in Christ," visit www.ficm.org/whoami.htm.

Spiritual Implications

The spiritual benefits of self-awareness are demonstrated in the biblical examples of Hannah and David. When we have an emotional attachment to God, honesty about our heart's desires and confession can bring us into an intimate, worshipful relationship with God.

Hannah

Those who mourn will be blessed. That's what Jesus said in the Sermon on the Mount in Matt. 5. Hannah, Samuel's mother, is an example of someone who expressed her feeling to God and received comfort—not to mention a delightful answer to her prayers.

Hannah's circumstances were similar to Sarah's. They were both stricken with the pain of infertility. Their husbands loved them but had at least one son with another woman.

We first meet Hannah in the Temple. She had come from her home where Peninnah, her husband's second wife, had treated her harshly with verbal assaults, probably having to do with her barrenness. Hannah had stopped eating. She was distraught and sought comfort for her soul, so she went to the Temple to talk with her Heavenly Father. She felt free to pour out her heart to the One who could change her situation. With earnestness and emotion, Hannah consecrated herself, reasoned with God, and pleaded for a child. Eli the priest only saw her lips move and thought she was drunk.

When she explained her reason for being there, Eli blessed her and sent her on her way with a joyful countenance. She did, indeed, conceive and bear a son, whom she acknowledged as a promise from the Lord. She vowed before God that he would be set apart like a Nazirite and no razor would touch his head. God had used Eli to affirm His own goodness and blessing. He had heard Hannah's prayer.

Hannah is characterized by her open and very emotional exchange with the Lord along with her devotion and gratitude to God. Hannah used her self-awareness—the pain she felt from infertility—to go before God and ask for a child. That connection with God was intimate. God took her seriously and answered her prayer.

In pain, we may go to God on behalf of ourselves or our loved ones. We may cry out to God, lamenting and explaining our need. We may even fast to seek God with fervor and diligence. Does that mean God will always answer our prayers the way we want? No, sometimes His answer is no. But if we listen for and seek Him diligently, Scripture says we will find Him (Prov. 8:17; Ps. 91:14). And that's where the intimacy is—in His communicating with us. When God speaks to us, we experience His goodness and comfort, and it causes us to worship Him in a deeper way. This intimate moment with God is a faith-building experience. Hannah's expression of her self-awareness before God brought her comfort in the form of answered prayer.

David

King David let the world in on his most personal thoughts and struggles when he recorded his conversations with God in Psalms. It's obvious he had self-awareness, revealing his deepest fears, loneliness, depression, feelings of abandonment, joy, ecstasy, and victory. These songs also reveal an intimate relationship with God. David was more than just knowledgeable about God; David made a connection with God by being honest about what he was thinking and feeling. He trusted God could handle his honesty because God had affirmed David.

There wasn't a thing David couldn't tell God. Emotionally, David was naked and unashamed before God just as Adam and Eve were before sin entered the world. Nothing was hidden. There were no secrets. And God loved it. He called David "a man after his own heart" (1 Sam. 13:14).

Intimate Confessions with God

David confessed before God as a contrite sinner to receive grace and mercy. He writes that when he kept secret sins to himself, his body wasted away. But when David confessed, he received much more than forgiveness.

> Yes, what joy for those whose record the LORD has cleared of sin, whose lives are lived in complete honesty! When I refused to confess my sin, I was weak and miserable, and I groaned all day long. Day and night your hand of discipline was heavy on me. My strength evaporated like water in the summer heat. Finally, I confessed all my sins to you and stopped trying to hide them. I said to myself, "I will confess my rebellion to the LORD." And you forgave me! All my guilt is gone" *(Ps. 32:2-5, NLT)*.

David received physical health and a joyful countenance when he was honest before God. And science shows the same can be true for us as well. Dr. James Pennebaker, psychology professor and author of *Opening Up*, has researched the effects of confession since the late 1970s. He found that trying to hide our thoughts and feelings is hard work and gradually undermines the body's defenses, placing us at risk for disease.[2]

People of various cultural groups and religions around the world seem to have an urge to divulge their secrets to someone whether it's a tribal or religious leader, a stranger on an airplane, a therapist, their diary, or Oprah. Pennebaker believes that important biological changes occur when we confess intimately, and a social bond is forged between the confessor and the listener. It's a way to proclaim trust in the listener.[3]

David's confessional writings certainly evidenced both the biological benefits and the bond he had with God. Many psalms record God's dialogue with David, God's affirmation and love for David. The result was more than a cognitive response to God's forgiveness. David had learned that there is more to this relationship with God than just going to Him to arrange, structure, and improve his life. Because David made an emotional connection with God through prayer, and because he recognized and experienced the kindness of God, he was able to worship with freedom, to express his love and gratitude to God.

Time Out: Talk About God's Goodness

Tell your children about God's goodness to you. Maybe you avoided a possible car accident or received a job promotion. Your perceived gift from the Heavenly Father could be simple—a magnolia tree that made it through the harsh Minnesota winter months to bring you joy one more year or seeing a cardinal in your bird feeder for the first time. These heartfelt delights can easily be personal gifts from our loving God who wants to pour out His love on us.

Help your children see how God has been good to them too. Use daily happenings to point out how God has protected and gifted them. You will affirm and teach them about who God is, how to recognize Him working around them, and an appropriate response of gratitude. You'll teach them how to begin to worship God.

Chapter 3 Endnotes

1. John Gottman, with Joan DeClaire, *Raising an Emotionally Intelligent Child* (New York: Simon and Schuster, 1997), 100.

2. J. W. Pennebaker, *Opening Up: The Healing Power of Confiding in Others* (New York: Avon Books, 1990), 13-14.

3. Ibid., 181.

Empathy

"Jesus wept" (John 11:35).
"Therefore, as God's chosen people, holy and dearly loved,
clothe yourselves with compassion, kindness, humility,
gentleness and patience" (Col. 3:12).

Beth's husband was killed in a car accident. When I (Pam) asked if I could do anything to help, she responded, "Yes. Could you call friends from church to help me organize and write out my thank-you notes?" I was happy to help in a tangible way. As the group gathered, it became apparent why Beth wanted help with that particular task: *There were more than 400 cards to answer!*

Friends were not afraid to say how they remembered Beth's husband, Bill. They were free to share in her suffering. Why wasn't I? I had a tight feeling all over. I usually felt this way when I wasn't sure what to say, especially when comforting people in mourning. That day I learned how beneficial those cards were to Beth. The insight alone helped move me away from my own discomfort.

Those of us who haven't experienced the death of a loved one have no idea what it is to suffer this separation. But that doesn't mean we can't sympathize. Our imaginations allow us to both sympathize and empathize with others. In fact, sympathy and empathy are positive emotional reactions—they allow us to focus on another person by putting ourselves in his or her place and imagining how that person might feel, think, and act.

However, there is another emotional reaction that is often confused with empathy—personal distress.[1] Instead of focusing on another person, personal distress focuses on self. The tight feeling I (Pam) had when called upon to offer my sympathies to Beth was personal distress. I didn't know what to say. And it was difficult for me to see her in so much pain.

The pain of personal distress is hard to tolerate. Instead of offering comfort to another as we do when we feel empathy and sympathy, we look for ways to comfort ourselves. Some of us come up with trite clichés or moral explanations for why unfortunate circumstances happen; some of us simply avoid dealing with the situation. This preoccupation with ourselves prevents us from connecting with others and showing empathy.

On the other hand, when we can tolerate our own emotional distress, we are free to reach out to others. This is what we want to teach our children to do eventually.

Time Out: Personal Distress Checkup

You witness a parent in a store yank an uncooperative child to his feet, yelling obscenities at him for his misbehavior.

On television you see a thin, malnourished, half-dressed eight-year-old lying in the dirt.

The local news reports that police found six children under the age of five abandoned with soaked diapers and dirty water, hungry and alone in an apartment.

You see an embarrassed person in the local grocery store checking out ahead of you without enough money to pay the bill.

What feelings stir inside you when you see these things? Are you more apt to

- push your feelings away and think about something else?
- overreact and set out to change the world?
- contemplate the feelings and, if possible, follow up with reasonable actions or words that minister to the hurting?

These are all viable options. Of course, we need practical emotional boundaries. If we just get irate and change channels each time we hear of some such injustice, we aren't helping anything. And if we consistently hide our pain, we limit our ability to empathize with and love others. But if we can hang onto the sadness, the righteous anger, the compassion we feel, and channel those emotions properly, we are driven to help and driven toward ministry. The ability to tolerate emotion without pushing it away or getting carried away by it is absolutely essential if we are to learn how to empathize.

Pushing Away

A common response among children is to neither tolerate nor manage but to _deny_ unpleasant feelings or personal distress, especially in situations beyond their control, such as their parents' divorce. When the hurt is deep inside, it is hard for children to tolerate the heaviness they feel—they believe they can do nothing to change the situation. The easiest way to avoid feeling crummy all the time is to tuck that grief away somewhere. Adults use this coping method too. We'd just as soon not feel sadness, anger, fear, or disappointment. But if we choose to avoid these emotions, the result can be physical, emotional, _and_ spiritual tribulation.

Overreacting

There are certainly differences in how well children manage their emotions. Some children react with high emotional intensity—they seem to be more shaken and sensitive to what's happening around them. Other children are relatively content, no matter what the situation.

Highly emotional children have a more difficult time empathizing with others. It's harder for them to put their personal distress aside. Their own needs and frustrations are often overwhelming enough that they fail to recognize what another person feels. But learning to manage our emotions doesn't mean we ignore personal distress. Instead, we learn not to let our personal distress distract us from empathizing with others. Take my (Pam's) situation with Beth. Once I was less preoccupied with my own discomfort, I could connect more emotionally with Beth. How did that happen? As it turned out, being asked to help Beth caused me to focus on something other than my own distress and allowed me to more deeply empathize with her. Also, when I saw what the cards meant to Beth, the insight helped me think differently about her loss and thereby act differently. The lesson is that we don't need to be slaves to our personal distresses. How do we teach that lesson to our children? We can use the everyday happenings in life to help our children make sense of what goes on around them.

Using the Everyday Happenings

I (Rachel) recently experienced sympathy, empathy, and personal distress all within a span of three minutes. My husband, daughter, and I were outside a toy store when we saw a four-year-old girl pacing in front of the store, crying. She looked at me and said, "Do you know where my mommy is?" I knelt by her and asked her name. "I'm Julia. Where's my mommy?"

My heart leaping to my throat, I told her we'd help her find her mommy. I asked if they'd been in the store; she said she thought so. I asked her mommy's name, but by this time, Julia was crying so hard she couldn't speak clearly. I got her to go into the store with me, intending to find a salesperson to help search for the missing mom.

As soon as we rounded the corner to the checkout, Julia ran from my side crying, "Mommy! Mommy! Mommy!" The startled customer at the checkout turned around in time to wrap the little girl in her arms. As Julia continued to cry, her mother looked at us. I explained we'd found her outside and she was asking for her mommy. I tried to comfort the now distraught mother who'd thought Julia was right behind her with her baby sister, telling her Julia had asked an adult for help. Julia's mom thanked us for helping, then turned her attention to Julia. Now calmer, Julia listened intently as her mother told her *never* to leave a store alone. As we walked away, I was hit with a mixture of emotions. Initially, I'd felt sympathy for Julia—how horrible to be lost. Then I felt empathy for her mother—what a feeling to find your child was lost and you didn't even realize she was missing. Then I felt a little personal distress—what if that had happened to me? And all this in the span of three minutes.

My daughter brought it up later as we left the store. "Mommy, is the girl OK?" We talked about how sad and scared Julia had been but how happy she was when she found her mom.

Calista was two and a half at the time, so we focused primarily on feelings, with a little reason thrown in for good measure.

I was intrigued by the effect this situation had on Calista. In the thick of the moment, perched safely on Daddy's shoulders, Cali had said, "Girl, are you OK?" And then to me, "Mommy, help her." She sensed that this one was bigger than she could handle with a hug. And she was obviously paying close attention.

Children can be taught to develop an *other-oriented perspective*, as we'll discuss later in this chapter. But we can also help them practice tolerating unpleasant emotions by talking through the everyday occurrences in life.

Psychologist and author Dr. Lawrence Shapiro suggests building a child's emotional tolerance by practicing staying calm in provoking situations.[2] I (Pam) had such an opportunity when I spent time with my competitive four-year-old niece and nephew. They were playing the card game Go Fish. Since their little hands couldn't completely cover their cards, we could easily see them. They were rather oblivious to it, but I knew what was going to happen. Leah saw what she needed in Nick's hand and, of course, asked him for it. He was angry about giving up a card and he wanted desperately to refuse her. Nick now had the chance to practice staying calm during this provocation. Reasoning with a four-year-old can help to minimize frustration, so I explained to Nick that games would be no fun if we all didn't play by the rules. Then we reasoned that when he asks Leah for one of her cards and she has the one he needs, he will want her to give it to him. Using reason with Nick was enough to help him practice staying calm when he was provoked. Reason and self-talk are ways to soothe ourselves in highly emotional situations. The thinking brain needs to speak truth to the emotional brain. It is the guard dog.

Time Out: Handling Personal Distress

Does truthful insight or self-talk, also known as reason, help soothe your personal distress? Write down recent opportunities you've had to help your children handle their personal distress with insight or truthful self-talk.

As a parent, seize these occasions to teach and reason with your children on a level they understand. Identify and acknowledge the frustration they are feeling so it's noticed and validated. Encourage and show them how to be respectful of others. And then move on with life. This kind of parenting takes time and energy. And it calls for consistent accountability from you and your child.

Common Mistake No. 1: Intervening

One of the biggest mistakes parents make is to minimize our children's distress. Somewhere many of us adopted the notion that we would bolster our children's self-esteem by giving them everything we never experienced, including protection from emotional pain. Let's face it, it's difficult to see our children suffer. I (Rachel) wanted to squash the first mean kid at the park who made my daughter cry. That's a natural gut reaction, but one that it's good to squelch. And I quickly learned that if I protect my daughter from all emotional pain, I'm stunting her emotional growth. Instead, we talk through painful situations so she knows how to handle herself. But it's hard to get past that first step because if our kids feel good, we usually feel good too. Who wants to interrupt that with a tough life lesson?

There are indeed situations that call for us to rescue our children. But many times these difficult situations can help shape our children's character. They are opportunities to practice healthy ways of coping with unpleasant circumstances that life continually throws at us.

Joyce Meyer, a world-renowned conference host, tells of a man who watched a butterfly struggle to get out of its cocoon. It moved about tirelessly in the stuffed cocoon, begging for freedom. The man finally had enough. He wanted to free it. He picked it up and tore the cocoon a little so the butterfly would have an easier time. The butterfly made its way out but just lay there, swollen, and slowly unfolded its deformed wings. What the man witnessed next was morbid. The butterfly was handicapped. It couldn't fly. Its wings looked terrible. What had gone wrong? The man's rescue attempt had handicapped the butterfly. It needed the struggle of getting out of the cocoon *itself* to strengthen and finish developing its wings. The last crucial period of growth was in the struggle and delivery.

In the same way, our children benefit and grow through their struggles. They experience reality and learn to empathize with the underdogs in the world. Struggling forces us to look upward —to trust God to work things out. Not that we *invite* such incidents nor welcome them, but rather than fix and rescue, we can trust God to use them in our children's lives.

Common Mistake No. 2: Overindulging

Another mistake is that many parents today—including Christian parents—have destructively made their children the center of their world by overindulging them. Some parents have distorted the God-given idea that children are a gift from the Lord. Taking it too far, they have protected their children from personal distress and put them on pedestals, thereby not allowing them to learn to empathize with and think of others. Take the case of Brad and Beverly.

Brad is a 38-year-old executive. His wife, Beverly, a real estate agent, now stays home with their two sons, Nicholas and Grant. They waited 10 years to have children, until their careers were established. Nicholas was born first, followed by Grant, 21 months later.

Brad and Beverly have life all planned. She will return to work after Grant is in school. Meanwhile, there are preschool interviews, museums and libraries, parks and quaint coffee shops to make life full and rich. And the perfect family vacation to a tropical isle. Let's listen in:

Enter Brad and Beverly, Nicholas and Grant. Each boy is carried by a parent. Mom and Dad also tote a double stroller, backpack, and diaper bag. Beverly loudly dotes on her boys as if they were the only ones within earshot.

As sunbathers quietly enjoy their books, Brad plays exuberantly in the middle of the walkway with 18-month-old diapered Grant. Brad doesn't seem to care if others need to pass by. Grant grabs his mother's camera to play with, hitting it hard against the ground.

"No, no, Granty," Dad admonishes mildly.

Meanwhile, Beverly can be heard from the pool several feet

away. "Kick, kick, kick, kick, kick—oh, Nicholas, you are a very good kicker." About now, everyone watching wants to throw up.

Next morning, the foursome appears at breakfast with stroller and baby gear. The active and hungry boys are strapped to their parents' laps—a lame attempt to control the chaotic meal that ensues. "Good morning, Mr. and Mrs. Smith. What lovely children you have here!" The ingratiating waiter introduces himself. Turning to Nicholas, he says, "And what does this young man want to eat this morning?" Beverly answers for him, "He'll have the fresh-squeezed orange juice with the eggs Florentine, and a side order of fruit. Do papaya and fresh pineapple come in the fruit today?" It sounds like she is ordering for a prince.

Brad and Beverly are crude examples of parents who over-indulge their children in their own self-serving lifestyle while the rest of the world goes unnoticed. Unfortunately, their children will likely grow up focused on themselves with limited abilities to empathize.

Some of life's cold realities that Brad and Beverly's children will have to face will be more difficult because their parents indulged them. Indulged children often have not learned to take responsibility for mistakes because they haven't had to. Their attitudes isolate them, and their identity development is hampered. A sense of entitlement, an "I deserve it" attitude, will likely interfere with intimacy in their relationships. Lest you think it's only with expensive vacations that we indulge our children, think again. The weekly Wal-Mart runs can have the same impact if we buy Junior a treat each time just because he asks for it.

The question remains, how do we go on family vacations, buy special treats at Wal-Mart on occasion, and still raise children who are considerate of others? There are three things you can do in your home:

Help your child recognize how others feel.

Help your child reach out to others.

Teach your child to listen to others.

Recognize How Others Feel

Empathy is relatively easy to teach children because God has given us an instinct to be empathetic—it just has to be cultivated and nurtured. In fact, it's unusual for a young child *not* to be able to experience what others are feeling unless he or she has been conditioned to do otherwise.

A child's emotional response to others develops during the first six years of life. It seems to hinge on the amount of physical affection a parent uses to comfort his or her child. According to British psychologist and founder of the Attachment Theory, Dr. John Bowlby, children whose distresses are soothed by holding, cuddling, and physical attention during infancy are more likely to respond empathetically to the distress of others when they are older. Consequently, children without this experience tend to feel "unconcerned about the troubles of others." Parental affection seems to be a key component to nurturing empathy.[3] Have you ever been in the church nursery or daycare where one baby was crying and then another, who seemed fine a minute ago, began to cry too? Is it a conspiracy? No. Infants can't completely distinguish themselves from their environments, so when one baby cries, another will interpret the distress as its own and cry with the first. Once these babies become toddlers, they've learned that they are separate beings. At this point, they can distinguish between another's distress and their own. Toddlers will often observe that someone else is "sad" or "crying." They can identify that the problem is someone else's and they can label it. By age six or seven, children begin to learn how to respond to another's distress with a hug, a Band-Aid, or by going to get Mom.

For example, if you and little Johnny see another child fall down and start to cry, direct Johnny's attention to the outcome of that fall: "Oooh, see the big scrape on his knee and the tears? That must hurt—just like the time you fell off your trike, Johnny." He can relate to that feeling. Immediately, he knows how to line up his experience with what he just witnessed. Johnny also knows what he needed to help him feel better. You can ask, "Johnny, how can we help him feel better?" This is a simple way to connect Johnny's head with his heart.

When we teach children awareness of others' feelings by pointing out verbal and nonverbal clues, we are teaching them awareness of their own personal feelings and the body sensations that go with them.

Some children are very good at reading the feelings of those around them. And these kids are often sought-after friends. It makes sense that they are well liked because they can pick up on what their friends feel and are likely to respond empathetically. They are more sensitive and less likely to offend others than a child who has not learned to pick up on the emotional cues from others. So is it any wonder that they are more successful not only in school but also on the job? By helping our children learn to read others, we are, essentially, teaching them to have an *other*-oriented perspective as opposed to a self-oriented one.

Reach Out to Others

Children learn by watching those around them. Toddlers are especially good at imitating what they see others around them doing. So it follows that the most effective way to teach empathy to our children is for them to see us in action.

Allow your child to see you cook a meal for or bring pizza to a family with a new baby or someone who is ill. Say to your child, "Now that the baby is here, Mrs. Brown will probably appreciate not having to make supper tonight. I know I would." Take your child with you to Mrs. Brown's to let him or her witness and feel Mrs. Brown's appreciation.

While your children are young enough to be fascinated, take them to a nursing home to read to a resident. Comment to them, "It must get awfully lonely in here every day without visitors."

Write a letter to Grandma, a shut-in, or a missionary family.

Instead of a family Christmas exchange, buy gifts for a less fortunate family in your community. Your local Community Action program would be happy to match you up with a family and their needs. Shop, wrap, and deliver together.

Take fresh vegetables out of your garden and bring your children along to give them to your neighbor. Tell them that Mr. Jensen doesn't have a garden, and he might consider it a real treat to have fresh food.

Volunteer to chaperone your daughter's junior high class trip to serve the homeless in a soup kitchen. This will broaden her perspective of hurting and needy people in the world. She will feel satisfied and worthwhile having made a contribution.

Take opportunities to help your children focus on others rather than themselves. As they mature, they will better understand how a person's circumstances may cause the person to feel, and they will be learning to read emotional cues. Having practiced responding with empathy as children, they are more likely to respond to another's pain or circumstances when they reach adulthood.

Be careful, however, not to make these opportunities chores or tasks, but rather gifts from your heart. Your kids will be able to read your attitude before they'll be able to fully understand your actions toward others. If you're delivering fresh vegetables to Mr. Jensen because it's a good learning opportunity for your child, your child will pick up on that and see it as a task. If instead you're delivering garden goodies to Mr. Jensen because you think he'd *like* them, great. It's a fine line, but one children can read. And if our attitude is wrong, we end up with cynical children rather than empathetic, caring ones.

Listen to Others

A third way to help children step outside themselves is to teach them to listen to others. This is best done by showing them how it feels to be listened to. When we *listen* to our children, we accomplish at least two things: We build a relationship with them, and we teach them how to listen to others. The Book of Proverbs tells us that one of the first steps in becoming a wise person is to listen.

"The wise also will hear and increase in learning, and the person of understanding will acquire skill and attain to sound counsel [so that he may be able to steer his course rightly]". (Prov. 1:5, AMP.)

There is a difference between hearing and listening. Sean Covey, in his book *7 Habits of Highly Effective Teens*, writes about genuinely listening to others with your eyes, heart, and ears. He says that listening with your ears isn't good enough because words only constitute 7 percent of communication. Our body language reveals 53 percent, and the tone and feeling in our voice communicates 40 percent of what we want to say.[4]

A good strategy is to practice *reflective listening.* For example, your son gets in the car after school. He looks mad, his body movements are abrupt, and his words are clipped. You say, "It looks like you're mad about something. What happened?" This tells him you've observed his feelings and are interested in him. Enough consistent responses reflecting what he said tell him he can trust you to listen without giving a lecture on changing his attitude and behavior. If he walks away feeling like he just heard a lecture, you'll communicate that you haven't heard him at all. By using reflective listening, we teach our children to read feelings in others and to respond accordingly. Remind your older children that they don't need to have all the answers or the right advice when they listen to their friends—reflection is worth a lot. And if you help them realize these truths in their own peer relationships, they'll start to make the connection in their relationship with you as well. They'll catch on that you may not have the answers all the time but your willingness to listen is often better than having the right answer.

Listening is a selfless act. Let's look at the story of Job in the Bible. You can find the whole story in the Book of Job in the Old Testament.

Job's Counselors

Job was a man who was "blameless and upright; he feared God and shunned evil" (Job 1:1). He was blessed with a large family and enormous wealth. Satan asked God to remove the hedge of protection around Job so they could see if Job loved God only because his life went well or if he would love Him under adverse circumstances too. Satan tested Job. He had the Sabeans steal Job's oxen and donkeys. They set fires and burned his sheep and servants. Then Satan summoned the Chaldeans to steal Job's camels and kill more servants. He brought a strong wind to blow down Job's house, killing his sons and daughters. If that wasn't enough, Satan next attacked Job's entire body with sores.

When Job's so-called friends arrived to comfort him, they were appalled at his appearance. They wept, tore their robes, and sprinkled dust on their heads as a symbol of mourning. For seven days and nights they sat by Job's side and said nothing. So far, so good. But they couldn't leave it alone. They set to figuring out the root of Job's problem.

It's important to understand the mind-set of Job's friends who became his "counselors." As Israelites, they believed that God is almighty and perfectly just. They also believed that no human is wholly innocent in God's eyes. Therefore, the logical conclusion was that every person's suffering was an indication of the measure of his guilt in God's sight. Why else would God allow bad things to happen to seemingly good people? Their orthodox theology heaped even more pain on Job's overburdened shoulders. His friends demonstrated little empathy. They thought Job was getting what he deserved. But in his heart, Job knew his godliness had not been self-serving.

Even with his friends at his side, Job was alone as he agonized. He didn't feel them next to him in spirit. It seemed to Job that God had deserted him, which was the most painful blow of all. And his friends affirmed the misguided belief.

None of Job's friends understood the benevolent grace of God, so how could they give it to Job? When true empathy is given to others, grace is also given, and the love of God is evidenced as fruit of the Spirit. Empathy is like healing balm on an open wound.

Spiritual Implications of Empathy

Scripture is clear that the most effective Christians are those who love others. One way that love is evidenced is through empathy. It's not what we say or how much we know; it is about emotionally connecting with others. When others know that we hear their pain and struggles and still accept and hang in there with them, powerful Kingdom work takes place. Jesus said that if we love others, then others will know we belong to Him. They will associate us with Jesus. He will be more real and credible to them. We draw others to us and to Jesus when we make emotional connections with them by using empathy.

Jesus—the Ultimate Empathizer

Jesus is our best example of someone who demonstrated empathy. Take His empathetic ministry to the woman caught in adultery (John 8:3). Jesus was teaching in the Temple courts. The Pharisees and teachers of the Law brought a woman to Him who was caught in adultery. They dragged her out into the street for Jesus to judge. The Pharisees wanted to know what Jesus thought about stoning her according to the Mosaic Law. Surely He would say to keep the Law above all else. She would have to be stoned, they thought.

Jesus knew the rejection this woman felt from the most important and powerful men in society. He understood it precisely —they were rejecting Him too. He loathed their self-righteousness, manipulation, and blindness to their own sin. So He answered by saying that if any of them was without sin, he could throw stones at her. When they left, and Jesus was alone with the woman, He didn't condemn her but told her to change her lifestyle for her sake.

Another good example of Jesus' empathy is the story of Lazarus' death (John 11). Jesus spent a lot of time with His friends Mary and Martha and their brother Lazarus from Bethany. Jesus was frequently a recipient of their hospitality when He traveled through their village.

Jesus was away when Lazarus became deathly ill. When Lazarus died, Jesus got word and waited until the fourth day to go to His friends' house. When Jesus saw the sorrow in Lazarus' sisters, Scripture says He was "deeply moved in spirit and troubled" to the point of shedding tears (v. 33). William Barclay, in his commentary on the Gospel of John, describes this moment as "one of the most precious things in the gospel. So deeply did Jesus enter into men's sorrow that his heart was wrung with anguish."[5] The people standing by observed that Jesus loved Lazarus very much to become so emotional. In this story, John shows us "a God whose heart is wrung with anguish for the anguish of his people. The greatest thing Jesus did was to bring us the news of a God who cares."[6]

Florence

There are those among us for whom the thought of Jesus' crucifixion is too painful. Personal distress prevents them from looking at what Jesus did for us. And because they can't seem to let in the reality of Jesus' gift, they miss out on grace. Florence is such a one.

As much as she hated to admit it, the Easter season was not Florence's favorite. In her church, an illumined portrait of Christ praying in the Garden of Gethsemane was above the altar's center. It was the custom on Good Friday to drape a black cloth over the picture to symbolize Jesus' suffering and death. It was meant to be a reflective part of the service. No one spoke; they watched and meditated. Florence never liked that part. She was relieved when Easter Sunday rolled around. She no longer had to be reminded by that black cloth of Jesus' suffering for her.

Florence couldn't _tolerate_ the negative emotions of thinking about the suffering Jesus endured for her sake. She couldn't bear to think of Jesus under the lash, being pierced by nails for her sins. Unfortunately, many of us are like Florence, at least to a degree. We have walls around our hearts that prevent us from understanding and appreciating what Jesus did for us. By not letting it get to our hearts, we are unable to receive the blessing of His love. As a result, we aren't able to see our sin for what it is. We unconsciously say to ourselves, "I didn't make Him do it. He didn't have to do that for me." We reject His gift, perhaps because of our own personal distress.

Have you ever noticed how much easier it is for children—naive as they may be—to accept this? Perhaps that is why Jesus told the adults listening to come to Him as a little child. He also asked us not to get in the way of children coming to Him. Somehow we, as parents, need to help preserve our children's soft spirits that willingly receive what Jesus did for them.

It is certainly the work of the Holy Spirit to penetrate our spiritual blindness and make us more like Jesus. But, as parents, we have some responsibility to help. We can give our children opportunities to become other-oriented instead of self-oriented. We can teach them to respect and listen to others in such a way that allows them to make an emotional connection.

We can encourage and help them learn to handle the pain of others and, eventually, possess the emotional tolerance to appreciate the reality of Jesus' suffering. This is the beginning of true worship and fellowship with the lover of our souls because our appreciation for what God has done spills out in our worship.

Chapter 4 Endnotes

1. Nancy Eisenberg, with Richard Fabes and Sandra Losoya, "Emotional Responding: Regulation, Social Correlates, and Socialization," in *Emotional Development and Emotional Intelligence: Educational Implications.* Ed. Peter Salovey and David J. Sluyter (New York: Basic Books, 1997), 142.

2. Lawrence Shapiro, *How to Raise a Child with a High EQ: A Parent's Guide to Emotional Intelligence* (New York: Harper Collins Publishers, 1997), 287.

3. John Bowlby, *A Secure Base* (London: Roultedge, 1988), 82.

4. Sean Covey, *7 Habits of Highly Effective Teens* (New York: Fireside, 1998), 171.

5. William Barclay, *The Gospel of John, Volume 2* (Philadelphia: Westminster Press, 1975), 97.

6. Ibid., 98.

5 Social Awareness

"Let our lives lovingly express truth [in all things, speaking truly, dealing truly, living truly]. Enfolded in love, let us grow up in every way and in all things into Him" (Eph. 4:15, AMP.).

Narcissus

Some would argue that we live in a narcissistic society—we are rather consumed with our own needs. The word *narcissism* comes from the story of Narcissus, a mythological adolescent who was extremely handsome.

As the story goes, a young nymph named Echo fell in love with the self-absorbed Narcissus. But she, being cursed by Zeus's wife, Hera, could only echo words that were spoken to her first. As a result, she couldn't express her love to Narcissus unless he first expressed his to her, which he never did. Instead, Narcissus spurned Echo's affection and she died of a broken heart.

The gods punished Narcissus for his callousness by making him fall in love with himself. One day he noticed his reflection in a pool of water. He was so enamored with his good looks that he couldn't leave the reflection and so died there. Narcissus' punishment—not being able to love another—came because he forsook the pure delight of sharing himself and his love with someone else. He never learned to notice another's pain or joy because he was so caught up in himself.

So it is with those stricken with narcissism. Their primary

goal is to protect their own images, leaving them unable to empathize with others. They may appear to be caring, but only if it will enhance their own images. They are consumed with themselves to the exclusion of others. Those who have *self-awareness* (as we discussed in chap. 4) are able to love themselves and others because they know who God created them to be. Sometimes, a keen dose of self-awareness is mistaken for narcissism, but they aren't the same. A person who is self-aware is also able to focus on others. A narcissist is not.

That said, all of us have gone through at least one narcissistic phase in our lives. The first comes in infancy. Newborns are aware only of their own needs. They don't even realize other people exist until they are several weeks old. That, of course, is "healthy" narcissism. Most of us go through a second bout of narcissism in our adolescent years. The measuring stick for doing most anything is, "How will it make me look?" Go to the mall by myself? No way! I'll look like I don't have any friends. Go to the movie with my parents? No thanks! I'll look like a loser! For the average teen, life revolves around self. For parents, this can be an especially difficult period. But there is hope! A parent educator I (Rachel) know tells parents that the teenage years are a flashback to the terrible twos. Think about it. Two-year-olds are just figuring out who they are apart from Mom and Dad. They are gaining more control over their bodily functions. They are learning to deal with a wide range of emotions. The result often looks like a temper tantrum but is really a confused child trying to sort out new emotions and physical changes. Fast-forward 10 years. The terrible twos are a distant memory. We can even laugh at some of our youngsters' antics—after all, they are a thing of the past. Or are they? As adolescence begins, a child's body is going through all sorts of changes. Hormones are raging. Some days the adolescent feels like an adult; others days, he or she acts like a child. It's tough for adolescents trying to find a place in this awkward in-between stage. The problems are actually quite similar to the problems faced at the age of two. The kid is bigger now, so often the tantrums are too.

Fear not! Just like the terrible twos, this is only a phase. Sooner or later the adolescent moves into early adulthood—out of a focus on self and into a focus on others. Your adolescent is becoming _other-oriented_. But be warned: This isn't some magic overnight transition. Just as we help our two-year-olds learn to deal with emotions and bodily functions, we need to help our adolescents learn to see themselves in a world where other people have equal value. We need to teach them to abandon those "entitled" thoughts and feelings of adolescence. And just as they craved structure when they were toddlers, they yearn for it now. It's our job as parents to help them break out of the narcissistic attitudes of adolescence.

Reading Social Cues

Being aware of how others feel is the first step in making connections with them. Do you remember any of your own social faux pas growing up? You know now that there are some things you just don't do. But how did you find out what they are? We all learn by trial and error to some extent. But having a loving coach for a parent—one who doesn't shame—is the ideal.

When my (Rachel's) brother-in-law, Steve, was four, there were an unusual number of deaths in their congregation. Naturally, Steve had all kinds of questions, the key one being, _What makes people die?_ His mother carefully explained that some of the people had been very sick, others had been in bad accidents, and some were just very old. One day, at the grocery store, Steve was walking down the aisle ahead of his mother and brother. An elderly lady, crooked and bent, made her way slowly down the aisle toward him. Steve beamed as he said quite loudly, "Look, Mom! This one's just about dead!" Now, some 40 years later, this is a fun family story. At the time, however, Steve's comment mortified his mother. And it presented her with an opportunity to clarify her comments about death and to keep a dialogue going with her son.

Was Steve's comment offensive to the elderly lady in question? Not terribly. Fortunately, she didn't understand its context. And many a four-year-old has said more inappropriate things. It's at these times we want to turn to the next shopper in the aisle and say, "Whose kid is that?" Instead, we are called upon to gently instruct our children so they become socially aware. Had

Steve's mom made him feel ashamed of his comment, she could have confused him and closed the door on that learning opportunity.

Time Out: Teaching Teens

Inappropriate comments from cute four-year-olds are one thing. Have you ever watched an opinionated adolescent spout off about a subject on which he has incomplete information? You feel embarrassed for him. Truth be told, he is probably pretty embarrassed, too, when he doesn't get the response he was looking for. But he, too, needs a parent who will coach him, not shame him. That's *so* much easier to say than to do. Adolescents can wear on your nerves like nothing else. You feel like you can gently instruct only so many times before you'll explode. So here's our challenge: When you're ready to yell at your teenager for the umpteenth inappropriate comment, stop. Picture him or her as a two-year-old and remember that the brain and body are going through many of the same growing pains now. Then help your teenager think through how the comment made others feel and how it could have been said differently. Eventually, your teen will catch on. But if you yell or use shame, you'll be tuned out and your opportunities for real instruction will be few.

It takes time to interact with our children. But that's the only way to proactively teach them to sum up social situations. It's an ongoing lesson, starting with that first embarrassing comment in the grocery store. Daily life offers plenty of opportunities to help our children become aware of what is going on around them and how their behavior affects others.

Reading social cues is only the first step. *Responding* is the next. Again, we can use daily occurrences to teach our children common courtesies. If our children know and show appreciation, if they can apologize and forgive, and if they are able to evaluate give-and-take in their relationships, they are well on their way to becoming *other-oriented* and making an impact in the lives of others. They are also more likely to identify and pursue healthy relationships with others.

Where do we start? By practicing these skills ourselves. We can practice and teach with three simple phrases: "Thank you,"

"I'm sorry," and "How are you?" The attitudes fostered by these phrases feed our relationships with others and with God.

"Thank You" (Appreciation)

It was Christmas Eve and six-year-old Nick couldn't wait to give Grandpa his special gift. Nick had picked out the screwdriver all by himself and had paid for it with his own 50¢. Nick imagined that Grandpa would be very pleased with his gift. Watching Nick's anticipation as Grandpa carefully unwrapped the gift was priceless. Grandpa saw Nick's excitement and responded with love and appreciation. They had connected on an emotional level. Grandpa even sent Nick a special thank-you note for his wonderful gift.

If Grandpa had carelessly unwrapped the gift or made a comment about how cheap it was, or neglected to thank Nick, he would have built a wall between himself and Nick. If we don't read emotional *cues* from others such as the excitement in Nick's face, or know how to respond appropriately to social cues, in this case, with gratitude, we will alienate ourselves from others and hurt them. That is especially true with children.

For the most part, we live in a culture that believes it is entitled to the good life: "I deserve this because I earned it or just because of who I am." Where a spirit of entitlement exists, appreciation and graciousness do not. But an attitude of gratitude goes a long way toward making connections with others. And any child who has a gracious or thankful spirit shines in our world. Here are some practical ways we can begin early to instill gratitude in the heart of a child.

Teach Appreciation

"Jimmy, tell Grandma 'thank you' for the nice birthday present."

"Sarah, tell Aunt Sandy 'thank you' for having us over today."

How many times have you had to coach your children to thank someone? Does it feel like you're getting a performance out of them instead of heartfelt gratitude? When they're young, it will. Eventually, it will become second nature. Jeff and I (Rachel) made a conscious effort to be polite with Calista so she learned quickly to respond in kind. Now I get comments all the time from other adults about how polite she is and how enthusiastic she is about even the smallest of gifts.

There are many ways you can foster an attitude of gratitude in your child. Here are two to get you started.

Get your child in the habit of writing thank-you notes for gifts. At first you might be the one doing all the writing. Then you may write the note but have your child sign his or her name. Eventually, have your child write simple sentences—even just two on a note card. It doesn't have to be elaborate. The reader will be touched by your child's efforts.

Act on your own feelings of gratitude. There is a chain of restaurants that my (Rachel's) family frequents. One of the franchises near us is always immaculate—the floor gleams and the bathrooms sparkle. I so appreciate having a clean rest room in a restaurant, especially with a potty-training toddler in tow, that I felt compelled to tell someone. Usually, when you ask to speak to the manager of a restaurant, it's to complain. I love to tell managers when they are doing a good job—it takes them by surprise and always elicits a smile. Children see this and learn that it makes people feel good when you thank them for their efforts. This is actually an example of modeling—read on.

Model Gratitude

Have you ever gone out to eat with your family and in front of everyone thanked the person who paid for the meal? Almost everyone followed your lead, right? Let your children hear you say "thank you" to them for the favorable things they do and say. "Thank you, Katie, for getting a rag and cleaning up that mess on the floor." Let your children hear you thank a grocery store clerk, the barber, your spouse, your mother. More than likely, they will follow your lead. We all love being appreciated.

Maybe affirming others isn't a natural part of your personality. Or maybe being around people who are positive *all* the time makes you crazy. We're not talking about ignoring or candy coating the messes in our lives. But there is always something to be thankful for, even if it's just being able to get out of bed in the morning. Give yourself an attitude check. You can make a conscious choice to be more positive, more thankful, more affirming. And making that choice can change your emotional outlook, how others react toward you, and how you perceive yourself. Modeling a spirit of gratitude to our children infuses the same in them. It's powerful!

"I'm Sorry" (Reconciliation)

This side of heaven we are going to offend one another—most of the time, unintentionally. By virtue of being human, we are not always going to say or do the right thing. We will read people and situations wrong from time to time. But God has given us a plan to work out our differences and be reconciled to one another. Two powerful words will put life back into a relationship: "I'm sorry." They are absolutely essential in our relationship tool kit.

But this phrase doesn't get the airtime it once did. Saying "I'm sorry" makes you vulnerable. You are putting yourself at another's mercy—not an easy place to be, especially in our "look out for number one" world.

The consequences of _not_ saying "I'm sorry" are many:

- Family members get into disputes and end up not speaking to one another for years.
- Marriages fall apart.
- The workplace is dreadful instead of fulfilling.
- Parent-child relationships go sour.
- Friendships dissolve.
- The cause of Christ is damaged.

Wait—what was that last one? What does my saying "I'm sorry" have to do with the cause of Christ? Plenty. Christians live in fishbowls—everything we do is scrutinized by those who would prove our beliefs false. There's some pressure for us to put our best foot forward—to look good and seem like we have it all together. So we avoid addressing the real problems in our lives. But if the real problems aren't on the table, apologies and forgiveness don't stand a chance. Without humility, the world considers us self-righteous and arrogant. And we are. Which brings us to the cause of Christ. We are sinful human beings. There's no getting around that one. But Christ died and rose again that we might be *forgiven* and have new life in Him. And He challenged us to forgive others as we have been forgiven. When we do that, the world sees us for who we are, damaged goods made well by our loving Savior, Jesus. When we say "I'm sorry," we are living out God's command and opening doors for others to learn of His love.

The perception is that saying "I'm sorry" puts you in a bad position—one of humility. Admitting you're wrong automatically puts someone else in the right. But the perception is backward. Saying "I'm sorry" is amazingly freeing. It releases you from all the garbage of holding on to your sin.

You can generate much freedom in your family life by using apologies when they are due. Let your children witness you, as parents, apologize to each other and to them. If you lose it over spilled milk, make sure you apologize to your child for the way you handled the situation. Children are quicker to forgive than anyone. They will usually even try to console us when we apologize for something: "That's OK, Mom." The irony is that we are more credible in our child's eyes if we admit when we're wrong. It is by this example that a child begins to understand that he or she is not perfect and that there is a way to make wrongs right.

If your children have a safe environment to admit their wrongdoings because they have experienced forgiveness and reconciliation from you, they have the foundation for understanding God's forgiveness and reconciliation as well. What a gift that is.

On the flip side, if children grow up in a home where parents don't admit mistakes, they gain a negative impression of themselves and don't see their parents as real people. My (Rachel's) brother-in-law and sister-in-law instilled a spirit of forgiveness in their children early on. For years, they have told their children, "We will always love you and you can always come home." Isn't that what Christ says to us? An attitude of forgiveness is essential to a child's spiritual well-being.

Model Reconciliation

Your humility can speak volumes to your teens too. Last year, the Lord asked me (Pam) to reconcile with a particular person I knew I had hurt. I planned to go quietly to speak to her. My 18-year-old daughter wanted a ride to the store, so I told her I'd drop her off at the store and pick her up in a bit. "But why aren't you coming?" I told her I needed to go talk with someone. "Who? Why?" I told her God had asked me to apologize to this person for hurting her awhile back. That's all I said. Of course, when I picked her up at the store, she was interested in how it went. I told her it went beautifully. Being forgiven and reconciled to an old friend is a wonderful thing. My teenage daughter was touched just as I was. She saw what "I'm sorry" can do.

Teach Reconciliation

When your children are old enough to communicate verbally with you and you are teaching them that something they are doing is hurtful to someone else, ask them to say they're sorry. Walk them through the process of apologizing. When my (Pam's) children fought, it became routine for them to say a quick "sorry" to avoid consequences. The amount of remorse in those flippant childhood apologies is debatable. One mother even told me her little girl said she was sorry so much she didn't know what she was apologizing for at times. To help her child think about what she is apologizing for, the mother starting asking questions like, "What are you apologizing for?" so she names the specific offense. And "Do you see how that hurt Jack?" so she acknowledges the hurt it caused someone else. True repentance involves change. Granted, the offense will probably happen again, but our children need to be taught that when we are truly sorry, we commit to not doing it again. And that knowledge may help them avoid relationships with unsafe people who apologize but don't change their abusive behavior. The sooner our children are adept at repenting, the better. If they can admit when they are wrong, they will minimize a spirit of entitlement and make their relationships safer and stronger. It's freeing to be able to admit when we're wrong and to move on.

Practice the moving on part yourself. When a child has apologized and you have offered forgiveness, that offense is over and done with. Let it go. Assume it won't happen again. If it does, deal with it then. But forgiving includes letting it go. God tells us that when He forgives our sins, He forgets them as well. He doesn't keep a logbook of our offenses to read back to us. It's important for us as parents to model His example of forgiving and not bringing it up again.

Time Out: Practice Apologizing and Forgiving

Does your family make it a practice to apologize to one another? Review the three elements of an apology: (1) Say, "I'm sorry" for a specific offense. (2) Acknowledge how it hurt. (3) Make a commitment not to do it again. Practice these steps yourself and your children will soon follow your lead. If they are very young, they'll need some guidance. Older kids may need gentle reminders.

After you've worked on apologizing, work on the flip side— forgiving. Kids often think in black and white and keep a mental tally of others' wrongs. Take some time as a family to talk about the "letting go" part of forgiving. Take a moment right now to read Heb. 10. Reflect on how great the Father's love is for us that He forgives and forgets. "'Their sins and lawless acts I will remember no more.' And where these have been forgiven, there is no longer any sacrifice for sin. . . . Therefore . . . let us draw near to God with a sincere heart in full assurance of faith, having our hearts sprinkled to cleanse us from a guilty conscience and having our bodies washed with pure water. Let us hold unswervingly to the hope we profess, for he who promised is faithful. And let us consider how we may spur one another on toward love and good deeds" (Heb. 10:17-19, 22-24).

Pray for your child's heart—that it would be soft to repent when necessary. And pray for yourself—that you would "remember their sins no more" and "spur" your children on "toward love and good deeds."

How Are You? (Give-and-Take)

"How are you?" is one of the most overused rhetorical questions in our language. It used to be that when you asked someone, "How are you?" you politely waited for a response and an actual conversation ensued. Now, it's polite to say "Great" or

"Fine, thanks," or something else innocuous since the questioner isn't really interested in a truthful answer. But at its root, this question represents something much bigger than a mere pleasantry. It moves people outside of themselves enough to think of others. That's an important step for children to take.

There's an old comedy sketch where a diva, after a long-winded story of her life, says, "Enough about me. Let's talk about you. What do *you* think of me?" We laugh because she's so caught up in herself. But inside we're thinking, "That reminds me of so-and-so. She only talks about herself. She never asks how I'm doing." Most of us have at least one of those relationships. They are completely one-sided and leave us tired because there is no reciprocity, no give-and-take in verbal or emotional exchanges. Emotional intimacy can't happen here because it requires that each person move outside himself or herself enough to learn about the other.

Intimacy means you know someone else so well that you are in tune with his or her very personal thoughts and feelings. This knowledge usually comes from in-depth communication on a multitude of topics. The more you know this person, the dearer you are to one another. You have made a connection. But connecting takes two, and when only one person shares feelings, seemingly not interested in the thoughts, feelings, and actions of the other, intimacy is impossible.

If we allow our sons and daughters to continue in an "it's all about me" mentality, they will be alienated from others. Their egocentric attitude will erode their friendships, marriages, and work relationships, and they'll never get past the "please give me" stage with God enough to know Him and worship Him and be intimate with Him. We can teach our children early on to have reciprocity—give-and-take—in their relationships.

Model Reciprocity

When my (Pam's) niece, Leah, was five, we went to the grocery store to look for flowers. Leah was greeted by an adult she knew. Leah responded and pretty soon I heard her say, "How's Claire today?" Claire was Leah's friend from preschool, I later learned. It took me by surprise—you don't often hear five-year-olds ask about their friends this way. Leah was imitating some-one. Her mom admits she didn't consciously teach Leah to ask about others but as Leah watched her mom take an interest in others, she learned nonetheless. You've probably made meals for the sick, sent cards to hurting people, verbally encouraged oth-ers, helped your next-door neighbor, or done something else to help others in need. As your children have watched you, they have learned. By watching you help others, they are learning that the world doesn't revolve around them.

Teach Give-and-Take

When our son (Pam's and Randy's), Michael, was old enough to talk with people, he would shun them in church. He was a "so-cially shy" kid. We coached him Sunday mornings before church: "Mike, this morning Pastor Tom is going to say hi and try to talk with you like he usually does. We want you to shake his hand and say hi when he greets you." This was a very basic way to re-ciprocate. Eventually, we worked on helping him make conversa-tion with others and look them in the eye. When children see that they can generate positive feedback, they feel good about their abilities to relate to those around them.

You can begin to teach children how to give in relationships early on. Brenda was getting ready to go shopping when she heard her three-year-old daughter, Kylie, greet her with, "You look pretty today, Mom." That was a pleasant surprise for Bren-da, but it needn't have been. Brenda was in the habit of tossing out affirmations to those she knew and loved. Kylie had been listening. Even as egocentric as three-year-olds can be, they can be taught how to reciprocate in relationships. Kylie's affirmation was one way to initiate a conversation with her mom. Asking questions is another way. When your children get older, help them learn to ask questions, especially ones that begin with *How . . . ?* or *What do you think about . . . ?*

Evaluate Relationships

Help your children evaluate the give-and-take in their rela-tionships, especially if you allow them to date. If your children are used to talking as well as listening in their relationships with you, they are more likely to recognize a relationship that lacks balance. Help them evaluate: Are they doing all or most of the talking? All or most of the listening? When they share their thoughts and feelings, do they feel listened to and understood? Do their dates argue too much? If you help them evaluate how they are being treated, they'll have a better understanding of how they are treating their dates as well. This is an invaluable skill—one that will help them as they approach marriage. Many marriages break up because the husband and wife never figured out how to balance the give-and-take. As a result, the relationship is plagued with misunderstandings that foster resentment, which builds into anger, and the cycle just gets worse.

If you have a compliant or shy child, he or she may need some help learning to both give and take in relationships. Such a child can be reluctant to tell you what he or she needs and wants. Consequently, the child can get stepped on by more aggressive children. He or she also may have a harder time expressing opinions and feelings. As a result, emotional intimacy is often lost because no one finds out about who the child is.

Time Out: Highs and Lows

You can help your compliant or shy children by drawing out their thoughts and feelings about their relationships. Use the dinner-table exercise "Highs and Lows." Each person takes a turn talking about the high point of his or her day as well as the low point. Talk about the feelings associated with both. Then pray for one another, thanking God for the high points and asking for His guidance with the lows. "Highs and Lows" works well with older children. For younger children, try "What Was Your Favorite?" I (Rachel) learned this from my sister-in-law and her family. At dinner, Mom or Dad asks, "Adam, what was your favorite thing at school today?" This practice "conditions" the children to put a positive spin on their day. They know they'll be asked for a favorite thing at dinner, so they think about it all day. Many days, they can't wait to share their favorite experiences. And dinner guests are included in the fun too. Dinner is an uplifting experience in that household. It can be in yours too.

Spiritual Implications

When you think about your best relationships (with your spouse, parent, child, relative, or friend), what is it about your interaction with that person that makes it satisfying for you? Check all the answers below that apply.

☐ We trust each other.
☐ We provide physical, spiritual, and emotional care for each other.
☐ We spend quality time together.
☐ We talk.
☐ We laugh.
☐ We look forward to being together.
☐ There's "chemistry" between us.
☐ We exchange ideas and learn from each other.
☐ We listen to each other.
☐ We like doing many of the same things.
☐ We respect each other.
☐ We respect each other's gifts and uniqueness.
☐ We are interested in what's new with each other.
☐ We hurt for and rejoice with each other in painful and joyful circumstances.
☐ We care about what happens to each other.
☐ We love each other.

Look back at what you checked. Notice anything? There is a mutual exchange in these activities—give and take. So it can be with God. His sovereign choice is to commune with us. He wants us to feel His love and to love Him back. There is heavenly value in knowing how to reconcile, appreciate, and reciprocate.

When we humbly reconcile with God with truly repentant hearts, an intimate bond develops. Ps. 32:1 tells us, "Blessed is he who has forgiveness of his transgression continually exercised upon him, whose sin is covered" (AMP.). When we are open to God's forgiveness because we have experienced it in our families, we see God as safe, kind, and forgiving. We are more apt to turn to Him in good times and in bad. We can't help but *worship* Him.

The heavenly value of an attitude of gratitude is a little more obvious: We are grateful for what God has done, namely the sacrifice of His Son, Jesus, so that we might have a relationship with Him. When we are able to receive what God has done with gratitude, our lives change. We accept and cherish His free gift, acknowledging that we could never pay for it. And because we are grateful, we respond with good deeds. This is true worship. The converse is good deeds that are performed in an effort to *earn* God's favor—something we could never do.

Finally, our ability to read social cues and respond with grace further advances the cause of Christ and gives us opportunities to present Him to others. Queen Esther and Daniel were two young people God used to win the favor of kings and change the course of history. They possessed wisdom and diplomacy in dealing with people without compromising their loyalty to God.

Queen Esther

A teenager taken into the royal court as a queen candidate, Esther used her social awareness and noble character to win the love and favor of King Ahasuerus. She was adept at reading people and situations, and responded diplomatically without compromising her faith in God.

Queen Vashti had refused to submit to the king, so he divorced her. That put him in the market for a new queen—someone who was beautiful and would submit to him.

When Esther met the king, he "loved her more than any of the other young women. He was so delighted with her that he set the royal crown on her head and declared her queen instead of Vashti" (Esther 2:17, NLT). There was something more to Esther than physical beauty. She was humane. She had mystique. She treated others with respect, which won her the respect of others. She also had self-control. The situation she faced required wisdom and strategy, and she was up for the task.

Esther's Jewish nationality was unknown to the king. Soon after her appointment as queen, she learned the king's right-hand man, Haman, was plotting to eliminate the Jews. She was now in a position to do something about it. Instead of reacting immediately and rashly, she fasted and prayed. She drew her strength and wisdom from God before risking her life by approaching the king. Her self-control allowed her to keep her emotions in check.

After three days, Esther dressed in her royal robe and stood outside the king's throne room to be recognized by him. Because she had won his heart through her respectful approach, he gladly invited her in and offered to give her any request up to half his kingdom. Here was her chance! The door was open for her to make her plea for the Jews. But she waited and instead asked the king and Haman to dinner.

Curiosity piqued, the king and Haman enjoyed a sumptuous supper with Esther's personal touches. The king wanted to know Esther's request. A perfect time to disclose her heart, you'd think. But again she waited. Did she know that God needed more time to work in the king's heart through a dream? Was she that perceptive? Did she know the voice of God in her spirit well enough to wait?

The next day, she again invited the king and Haman to a banquet. Then Esther exposed Haman's plot to kill the Jews. The king gladly granted Esther's request to save the Jews, and Haman died a traitor's death on the gallows he had prepared for the Jews.

We don't know specifically what made Esther so effective with the king and others in the palace, but they loved her. She knew the rules of her royal culture. She had studied the king from circumstances with Vashti enough to know what he didn't like. She managed her emotions and had respect for authority. She knew the power of prayer and fasting and used all these things sincerely to rescue her people bravely and admirably. Much like Daniel.

Daniel

As a 15-year-old, Daniel was described as a young man "without any physical defect, handsome, showing aptitude for every kind of learning, well informed, quick to understand, and qualified to serve in the king's palace" (Dan. 1:4). No doubt, it was these God-given qualities that helped Daniel survive his Babylonian captivity and win the favor of several kings throughout his lifetime.

While Daniel possessed social awareness and a sense of diplomacy and respect for others, he resolved to honor God before anything no matter what the cost. He had a way of doing *both* that most of us haven't been able to match. Several things made this happen for Daniel.

First, he didn't demand his rights or position but spoke to officials with such respect and sincere humility that he received their favor. The officials noticed Daniel's wisdom in how he spoke and what he said, and they probably appreciated how he made them feel about themselves. Whenever someone speaks to us respectfully, we feel valued.

Second, Daniel was not afraid to express loyalty to his God—who was different from the king's gods. His confidence in God was seen as commendable. He even went to the lions' den for it and was spared. There is something admirable about people who live by their convictions respectfully even if they are different from ours.

Third, even the king came to honor Daniel and put him in a high position in the royal court because of the wisdom and good judgment he displayed. God chose to give Daniel wisdom and good judgment for the lifelong assignment He had for him in Babylon. God used Daniel to bring glory to himself in a pagan society. That's one of the benefits of being socially aware—God brings glory to himself through us. Daniel's winning combination of love for God, respect for himself and others made him one of the most admirable men ever written about.

Time Out: Read Together

Read the stories of Daniel and Esther with your children. Read directly from the Bible or, if your children are young, from an appropriate picture book or children's Bible. (See Appendix D for suggestions.) Talk about the qualities Daniel and Esther displayed that made them so likeable and successful.

6 Motivation and Persistence

"Let us run with perseverance the race marked out for us. Let us fix our eyes on Jesus, the author and perfecter of our faith, who for the joy set before him endured the cross, scorning its shame, and sat down at the right hand of the throne of God" (Heb. 12:1-2).

Columbus's Journey

In 1482, Christopher Columbus wrote to a friend about a dream he had. He had learned about the East from Marco Polo's travels and thought it was possible to sail from Europe to China by a new route. He reasoned that if China was as large as Polo said it was and if he sailed east, he would surely run into it. He had no idea that another continent lay in the way.

Columbus was not deterred by tales of mysteriously calm and boiling waters or monsters that lived in the deep. His love for the sea and his interest in navigation begged for a purpose. He came up with a twofold reason for his adventure: He was interested in finding wealth for himself and his country, and he wanted to convert other parts of the world to Christianity.

The challenge for Columbus was selling his idea to someone who would finance him with ships, a crew, and provisions. For 10 years he persisted at approaching kings and queens and the Spanish Commission. During that period, his wife died, leaving him a small son to care for. Even so, Columbus pursued his dream. Finally, Queen Isabella of Spain agreed to sponsor the expedition. Three ships, 90 experienced crewmen, and provisions set sail on August 3, 1492.

Columbus soon found that the same persistence he demonstrated in soliciting sponsorship was needed for the journey. Trade winds carried the crew for several weeks, but when the winds stopped, the ships stopped. The crew was frustrated and restless in their tight quarters, and eventually mutinied. When the winds picked up, the crew settled down. They had been at sea four weeks longer than any other exploration had ever been and there was still no land in sight. Finally, one of the Bahamian islands appeared on the horizon.

On the return trip, Columbus remained hopeful and persistent while the crew again grew impatient from being at sea longer than expected. They endured storms, leaky ships, separation, illness, and death. Even when Columbus himself was very sick, he was planning his next voyage back to the New World. He returned several times.

Motivators: Passion and Prize

It was passion and prize that motivated Columbus to go to the New World. His passion was an intense love of the sea. His prize was both money and a desire to convert others to Christianity.

Motivation comes from the heart. It's aroused by emotion, desire, and our will to do what we believe is right. Also, as Christians, our motives are shaped by what we believe God wants us to do. Motivation fuels the persistence needed to finish a task. Our calling may not be to persist at something as outlandish as discovering a new world. However, as parents of young children, our calling to persist in maintaining a household with a sense of stability can be almost as daunting. We face interrupted sleep, sickness that spreads throughout the home, wet beds, endless dishes and laundry, the physical demands of each child. We're also expected to meet the emotional needs of attention, love, security, and discipline and provide for spiritual and educational needs. It takes both passion and prize to stay motivated and to persist at good parenting. Much as these are necessary skills for successful parenting, they are essential for children to learn as well.

Time Out: Passion for Parenting

Sit down with your spouse and discuss your passion and prize for parenting. What would you like for your children physically, emotionally, spiritually?

What's to Gain?

What do our children stand to gain from acquiring and using motivation and persistence?

A sense of accomplishment. Without goals, we aim at nothing and hit nothing. Our sense of purpose and self-discipline is encouraged when we complete what's necessary to accomplish our personal goals. From a spiritual perspective, we can be assured that God has an individual plan for each child (1 Cor. 2:9-10). We are meant to live out that plan. It takes both motivation and persistence to abide in Christ just as it does to live out His plan for us.

An ability to overcome obstacles. Every day holds its own stumbling blocks, and we have our choice of reactions: We can quit or persevere. If we choose to persevere, we gain a confidence that makes us more likely to persist in other challenges. It takes a strength of character and a little practice. But this skill will make you and me better parents. If I persist with patience, my child will eventually learn to brush his or her teeth without my help. It will also see our children through adverse mental and physical circumstances. It will help them persevere in less than desirable jobs while they earn money for school, stick it out through difficult classes, maintain their marriage commitments when times are tough, and get out of bed in the midst of depression.

Grandma's Marathon

Every summer in Minnesota, a 26-mile race called Grandma's Marathon is held on the shores of Lake Superior. My (Pam's) sister-in-law, Niter, bravely entered the race one summer. It was not a casual decision for this first-time runner. Her goal was to finish. Her passion and prize? A prestigious Grandma's medal. Someday she would be able to tell her grandchildren that she had run in this race. And although she trained for it by walking and running several miles a day for months in advance, it was still a challenge.

On race day, it was a cool 70 degrees with 98 percent humidity. It was drizzly and the air was thick—not ideal conditions, but Niter was motivated by the prize at the end. She walked and ran for more than six and a half hours. The last 8 to 10 miles were difficult. Pain rippled through her hips and upper legs. Her shoes rubbed against her baby toenails, which eventually fell off. There were times when she wanted to quit. During the last 3 miles, each step took all her concentration. She claims it was the hardest thing she has ever done, and it was worth it. She had the taste of victory. It was not the ultimate victory of winning the race, but it was a personal victory because she captured her prize. It couldn't have happened without persistence.

Persistence to Finish

While persistence and motivation work together, they are not the same. Our motives can be conscious or unconscious influences that push us into action. It was having a Grandma's medal for her grandchildren that motivated Niter to run. It took *persistence* to endure the fatigue and less-than-ideal conditions. The very nature of persistence is that we are struggling *against* something—a physical obstacle, a friend's disapproval, a group's opposition, or even Satan and his minions. But the apostle Paul reminds us that the only way to reach the prize is to persist: "Remember that in a race everyone runs, but only one person gets the prize. You also must run in such a way that you will win. All athletes practice strict self-control. . . . So I run straight to the goal with purpose in every step. I am not like a boxer who misses his punches. I discipline my body like an athlete, training it to do what it should" (1 Cor. 9:24-27, NLT).

Paul encourages us to run our race—live our life—in such a way that our circumstances are brought under subjection, instead of our becoming subject to circumstance. In other words, the bad weather and the pain in our bodies are not obstacles that compel us to quit the race. More specifically, the fatigue and daily pressures of parenting are seen in light of our goal. When we consider our intense desire to raise strong and stable children who have a foundation to become all that God created them to be, the obstacles are brought under subjection of that goal.

What made Columbus pursue his dream for 10 years and endure the long journey? Passion, purpose, plodding, and prowess —much of which is mental and emotional. How do we help create these fixings for motivation and persistence in our children's lives?

Passion (Desire)

If you have ever attended your child's sports events, you might have noticed some players have the talent to play but lack the passion. The talent is practically hidden without the passion: the intense desire to retrieve the ball when it rebounds from the basket and to move it down the court. Having tasted sweet victory, a player with passion wants to win. Passion is a necessary emotional component to play with full potential.

How can we help stir passion in the hearts of our children? It goes without saying that some temperaments are more colorful, demonstrative, social, and energetic than others. Some of us are content to be mellow, rational, less aggressive. The latter category may take the hit for having less passion because we experience our emotions differently than the first group. Nonetheless, we can still have deep interests in things that motivate us.

Passion starts as a seed and grows. As parents, we can be significant in planting seeds of passion by stirring our children's curiosity.

When I (Pam) think back on the seeds of curiosity we planted in our children's lives, it happened because of conscious and unconscious efforts. Naturally, we talked about and visited places we loved. When my husband, Randy, was our son Mike's age, he lived and breathed basketball. He trained year-round to be able to play during the short season. He spent many hot summer afternoons working up a sweat playing ball. He knew when our daughters and son were old enough to play, he'd have to find a balance between encouraging them to love it like he did and letting them choose what sport to play. His encouragement and volunteer coaching helped create a desire in Mike to play basketball. The passion for the game continues to grow within Mike.

As a family, we marveled at beautiful sunsets and the bright moon and stars in the sky at night. All of our children, especially Erin, have a deep appreciation for astronomy and God's creation. In the summertime, she will lie under the stars at night and bask in the glory of the universe. We read books together and visited the library on a regular basis when they were young. Hannah, our oldest, is passionate about books and learning.

For you, it may be a love for history, fishing, camping, showing hospitality, or some other interest. It may be music that you play in your house, concerts you take your children to, instruments and lessons you buy to see if a seed will land in fertile soil and begin to grow into a lifelong love.

Time Out: Planting Seeds

What seeds of curiosity have you planted or would you like to plant in your child's life?

Purpose

"Amanda, what do you want to be when you are on your own?" I (Pam) asked a 14-year-old. "A pediatrician," she replied. "I want to help kids." *Praise God,* I thought, *this girl has a dream.* She has a biological mother who doesn't want her and an older brother who verbally berates and threatens her. She is a victim of sexual abuse. This young woman needs something to live for. Her passion and purpose are to help children who hurt—like she does.

If your passion is to play basketball, then your purpose is to play well and contribute to the team. If your passion is to play the violin, then perhaps your purpose is to play your best for an audience who will be entertained. If your passion is farming, then your purpose is to do it well enough to make a living at it. If your passion is to be a parent, then your purpose may be to do your best to raise healthy, godly children.

We all need a purpose for living. When we ask children what they want to be when they grow up, we're asking them about what purpose they want to fulfill. It's really kind of a silly question to ask a young child. But it gets them thinking and dreaming about what they could become. And like Amanda, dreams are the only things some children have to hang onto. Once solidified, our dreams become our focus, our goal. And our actions drive us toward the goal.

As parents, it's our job to convey to our children that God has a purpose in mind for their lives—something just for them. It's not like their brother's or sister's. It's unique and tailor-made. It will be something that they enjoy and get excited about. When we trust God to have our best interests in mind, life becomes an adventure rather than something we take great pains to figure out. We can be confident that we will be significant in the kingdom of God as we yield to Him.

The catch is that we must believe for ourselves that God has a purpose for us before we can encourage our children to trust God's plan for them.

Time Out: Encouraging Your Child

What do you and your spouse believe about God's purpose for you and your children? Do you believe God has your best interests in mind? In what ways do you encourage God's purpose in your child? What areas of interest and gifting do you see God has blessed your child with? How have you encouraged or steered your child in these directions?

Plodding

If we look at the world's best athletes, musicians, and academic achievers, we'll find that they have spent a painstaking number of hours practicing or studying to be good at what they do. In fact, the more hours they've spent, beginning in childhood, the better they are. They've experienced the mental practice of being under pressure to perform and compete at extremely difficult levels.

Think of the enormous mental pressure championship golfer Tiger Woods has overcome to hold all four major golf championship titles at one time—the Masters, the U.S. Open, the British Open, the PGA—at the age of 26. Tiger's father and fellow players agree that he is unflappable even when he errs. When he takes the lead, his ability to focus and persist brings victory. Both his mind and body are brought under subjection and conditioned to accomplish his goal to win.

Practically speaking, most of us will not be the parents of Olympic athletes or child prodigies who spend most of their childhood practicing a talent to become a champion. However, to persist under adverse circumstances and overcome obstacles takes a resolve to not give up—a plodding, if you will. And everyone can benefit from having gumption.

Creating a strong work ethic in children is one way to develop persistence. It also helps minimize the fear of trying new tasks. Children and young adults who are not afraid of work have an advantage when it comes to accomplishing their goals. Whether it's studying for a final exam or helping the neighbor rake leaves in the fall, they can dive right in and get things done. They can bring circumstances under subjection and "just do it" easier than those who get bogged down mentally with "I don't feel like it."

Chores

We are strong advocates of having children help with chores around the house. For me (Pam), I learned to work in a family business beginning at age 10. My sisters, brother, and I worked in my dad's drugstore, sweeping the sidewalk before school, stocking and dusting shelves, and waiting on customers after school and on weekends. Unfortunately, we didn't learn much about how to work at home. Consequently, I had a crash course in doing laundry my first week away at college. My roommate didn't know either and someone had to teach us.

When I got married, I remember feeling overwhelmed with my part in managing the meals and cleaning because I didn't know how to get them done efficiently. It was one reason I wanted my own children to have some home management skills. Another reason is because their help around home is a contribution to the family. It's a way to give. It minimizes the entitled attitude of "It's Mom's job to clean while I watch TV." It's practice at persisting through jobs that aren't pleasant. And it makes children feel good about their follow-through abilities when they know how to do something, even if it's washing a window or folding a load of laundry. These are little successes that help build confidence to persevere at life's bigger tasks. To overlook this area is to invite sloth into a child's thinking and habits.

When our (Pam's and Randy's) children were small, we gradually introduced them to the world of work with the "job jar." It was a simple game we played five mornings a week in the summertime. The rules were:

Pick three pieces of paper out of the jar, each with one job written on it.

Do those three jobs before a designated hour in the morning.

You may have Sunday and one other day during the week off —your choice. It's a mini real-world experience!

The jobs were suited for their ages and, if they had never done the job before, I showed them how the first few times. My children quickly learned to empty the dishwasher, clean the bathroom sink, countertop, and mirror, put all the dirty clothes in the laundry room, vacuum the living room, sweep the porch. The jobs were reasonable and allowed them some freedom to choose to take the day off or do them later before the time expired. If they didn't get them done on time, two more jobs were added to their lists. When they finished their chores, the rest of the time belonged to them. The main thing is that the jobs were reasonable for their ages so they didn't become overwhelmed and discouraged. It's easier to start with less and add more than work with their disillusionment.

You can start having children help as early as age three or four with simple jobs like picking up toys, setting the table for a meal— with nonbreakables of course—bringing small bedroom garbage cans to the hallway where Mom can empty them, and so forth.

Encourage children that they are making a contribution to the family and blessing the family by helping and that they are learning skills they will need in years to come. Make it simple and fun by the words and tone of voice you use to teach the skills.

At my (Rachel's) house, Calista will announce, "This room's a mess! Let's clean it up!" Then she'll start to sing "The Clean-Up Song" she learned in Sunday School. I think a certain purple dinosaur on TV sings a version of this song too. So we sing while we pick up. The task is fun because we're working together and singing. It doesn't seem like a chore to Calista because she instigated it. It just doesn't occur to her three-year-old brain that this could be drudgery. It's my job to keep that fun, positive attitude going and apply it to other household tasks.

As a coach, you will need to show your children how to clean toilets, mirrors, sinks, and countertops. The challenge is to find something fun about each task. There is something appealing about using a spray bottle that made doing mirrors the most coveted job in our (Pam's and Randy's) home.

My (Pam's) girls were 8 and 10 when I showed them how to wash clothes, so I made it as simple as possible. I had the girls sort the clothes into two piles—lights and darks. And they were taught to use the same cycle on the machine so they knew where to turn the knob each time. I showed them how full to fill the baskets of clothes before dumping them into the washer, and how much soap to use. They stood on a stool to take the clothes out of the washer. Then they put them in the dryer on medium. They got it! And they were excited to wash clothes. If you're a perfectionist or have high-maintenance clothing, this method may not be for you, because there *are* some risks to your clothing. But teaching my children to do laundry was more important to me. In fact, now my girls are more particular about washing than I am. Best of all, they feel capable and independent.

Time Out: A Fun Work Ethic?

How do you encourage a strong work ethic in your child? Is it reasonable? Fun?

Prowess (Courage)

Some children get frustrated with their abilities and need extra encouragement. They tend to either expect too much of themselves or lack confidence. In either case, they are fearful, and the fear can be debilitating.

When I (Rachel) taught high school English, I had a student who was the worst speller I've ever seen. Karen's handwriting looked more like a 5-year-old's than a 15-year-old's, and there were days she didn't even spell her own name correctly. I thought it was laziness. At the beginning of the year, her attitude was that she wasn't going to try because she just didn't care. At the first parent-teacher conference, I shared my concerns with her mother. Karen's mom said Karen loved to write, so it surprised her that she'd have a bad attitude in English class. Her mom asked if I knew Karen had recently been diagnosed as dyslexic. Embarrassed, I said no. That explained the spelling problem! We talked a little more, and I came up with a plan. The next week, I quietly asked Karen to hang around after class, making sure it didn't look like she was being singled out for anything. I said, "I hear you like to write poetry. I'm a poet too. I'd love to read some of your work if you'd be willing to share it with me." She beamed and handed me a notebook. I promised to read it that night and return it the next day. Karen's poetry was magnificent. She had a gift for imagery and a real flair for phrasing. But writing poetry wasn't "cool" and neither was having a learning disability. This sophomore was trying desperately to fit in. She had let her emotions—and her need to be liked—get in the way of her learning. And I assumed she just had a bad attitude when I should have realized there was something deeper going on. As it turned out, Karen became one of my prize students. She grew in confidence and, by the end of the year, was joking about her spelling and sharing her poetry with the class. She led class discussions and shared her love of language with her peers. And wouldn't you know—her peers respected her for it.

In September, Karen had been emotionally overwhelmed. When that happens, it's as if the blood vessels in our brains constrict and we can't think rationally. The fear of not succeeding closes the doors to learning. We get in the habit of reacting with a flood of emotion and lose confidence in our own abilities. Like Karen, we need personal attention and coaching to learn to react differently. That's not to say that achievement and psychological testing don't need to be done to rule out other possibilities and modes of treatment. Remember, Karen had a legitimate learning disability that we had to work with too. Karen needed some success and some positive feedback to build her courage and confidence. Victory in this little battle was part of winning a bigger war—knowing she could overcome adversity when it came her way.

Spiritual Implications

What would motivate missionary Heather Mercer to pray, "Lord, send me to the hardest place on the face of the Earth?"[1] Her passion for adventure and for Jesus. She and Dayna Curry found purpose in ministering the love of Jesus to Afghan women and children in spite of the laws forbidding it. They became hostages of the Taliban government in Afghanistan for more than three months.

At the same time the world was praying for Heather and Dayna, we were praying for missionaries Martin and Gracia Burnham in the Philippines. They had been taken captive by a terrorist group who held them hostage for 376 days. In the end, a rescue attempt left Martin and a brave Filipino nurse, Ediborah Yap, dead and Gracia injured. How did the Burnhams and Ms. Yap hang onto their faith in God and their emotional wits in a jungle hideout, away from their young children for more than a year?

Gracia Burnham said, "We want everyone to know that God was good to us every single day of our captivity. Martin was also a source of strength to all the hostages. He was a good man, and he died well."[2] Martin and Gracia persisted in hanging onto Jesus because they were passionate about Him and about their purpose in God's kingdom. Martin did not fear death. He had premonitions of his passing and had already begun writing letters to his three children. He sang to his wife each night to comfort her. He persisted in his faith to the very end and used the grace God gave him to endure. His emotions of fear and longing for home were overshadowed by his passion for Jesus.

God may not be asking us or our children to be missionaries in life-threatening situations like the Burnhams or Heather and Dayna. But He does want our primary passion to be for Him. And He will use our passion to persist to do Kingdom work.

A Passion for Jesus

Dave Busby ministered to youth for more than 20 years. One of the questions he asked hundreds of young people across the country was, "If Jesus told you He wanted to have a personal conversation with you and sat you down face to face, toe to toe, knee to knee with Him, if He told you He had a very important question for you and that your answer was very, very important, what do you think He'd say to you? What would He feel about you? What would He communicate to you?"[3]

Dave put the youths' answers into four categories:

The first group thought Jesus would say, "Hey, I am so disgusted with you. You are ridiculous. I died on a cross, and you can't even read your Bible consistently."

The second group thought Jesus would be angry because they weren't doing the things they needed to be doing.

The third group said Jesus would be disappointed and hurt. He'd say, "You know, you have all been such a disappointment to Me. There is no way I can communicate to you how much you disappoint Me."

The last group said they had been such failures that Jesus wouldn't even pay attention to them.

These answers were from Christian students who were constantly made aware of their failure to measure up as "good" Christians. How can passion grow from that kind of seed? It can't. Children who think they are nothing but disappointments to God are missing out on the truth, which is that the Father loves and values them. An emotional attachment with the Father doesn't exist with those beliefs. As the apostle John writes, "How great is the love the Father has lavished on us, that we should be called children of God! And that is what we are!" (1 John 3:1).

Dave Busby told kids that he believed if they went head-to-head and toe-to-toe with Jesus, He would say to them, _"I have chosen you. I want you."_ Period.[4]

Our perception of Jesus and how He feels about us matters. It's key to building a connection with Him. Satan does not want us to know the truth of 1 John 3:1 because he knows that if we don't see ourselves as beloved children of God, we lack passion. And it's that passion for Jesus that gives us purpose—something to live and die for. It's what the Holy Spirit uses to empower us.

When we learn to trust and relate to a loving parent, we want to please that parent. The same is true in relating to God. When our passion is for Jesus, then our motivation is to obey and please Him. If obedience means sacrifice, the sacrifice may be easier if we've had practice overcoming physical and emotional obstacles like fear and depression. And a strong work ethic minimizes sloth and entitlement.

Emotional Persistence

Jamie is a 17-year-old boy who is known in his school for having a deep faith in God, but lives it rather quietly. He likes to have fun but has some strong convictions about teenage vices. He's not self-righteous and has an easygoing way of relating to believers and unbelievers alike. Jamie has self-awareness and empathy for others. He can pick up on how others are feeling based on cues and circumstances. And Jamie is comfortable with his own emotions when other people are hurting.

One day, Jamie found a note in his locker from a girl in his class. Though he didn't know her except to say hi in passing, she wrote to him because she thought his faith might help her. Jamie was pleased to share with her. As they corresponded through notes, Jamie came to learn that this girl's problems were more extensive than he was led to believe in the beginning. She was dabbling in the occult, depressed, and contemplating suicide. Jamie was burdened.

Most teens would be fearful of the emotional baggage Jamie had been handed. Many adults would be too. Jamie was emotionally competent, but that didn't mean this situation was easy to handle. Jamie did not jump ship. He involved others—his pastor and the school counselor for starters. He accompanied the girl to a meeting with his pastor. There they talked about the hope that comes from knowing Jesus. The girl did not act on the invitation right away, but Jamie continued to communicate with her, using appropriate boundaries.

Jamie's emotional skills allowed him to persist with this searching teen. If he had been afraid of his own emotions, he might have bailed out of the opportunity to share Christ. He might have run from the girl, causing her to feel rejected, reinforcing the shame and depression she was already living with.

The Apostle Paul

Saul thought he knew it all. His passion and zeal were for Judaism and the law. Jesus Christ and the Christians were his enemies, so he set out to destroy them and their cause. But God caused him to realize he was mistaken about his passion to serve God. He had actually been tormenting the very Lord he thought he was defending, as well as the Savior he had been waiting for. He was humbled on the road to Damascus by a blinding encounter with the living God (Acts 9).

His conversion to Christianity was dramatic and sudden. Jesus Christ became his passion. The spread of Christianity became his purpose. The Church grew in numbers and flourished in converts because of Paul's zeal. He is remembered as the architect of the gospel to the Gentiles, who, until he came on the scene, were not considered gospel-worthy.

Paul is a good example of motivation and hope. His conversion is a beautiful story of what God does when He makes us new creatures in Christ. The motivation and persistence with which Paul worked for the cause of Christ is praiseworthy. Though he faced danger, threats of murder, shipwrecks, stoning, beatings, prison, and rejection from his own race, he was not deterred from fulfilling his purpose.

Persisting in Adversity

The reality of this life on earth is that we will face loss and adversity. It may be living in a town or city that you don't like. It could be the death of a loved one. Some days will be hard. It's difficult to understand why God allows that to happen. And no one is exempt. The most devoted believers will experience difficult days.

Remember Job? His wife told him he should give up on God and suicide was the only way to get relief from his troubles. He told her, "Should we accept only good things from the hand of God and never anything bad?" (Job 2:10, NLT). How true that is for us as well. Our children will be watching and looking to us to help them cope when adversity strikes. We don't have to be superhuman by any means. But we need to model when and how to depend upon the Lord Jesus.

Chapter 6 Endnotes

1. Stan Guthrie, Zoba Guthrie, and Wendy Murray, "Double Jeopardy" in *Christianity Today* (July 8, 2002), 28.

2. Ted Olson, "Two Hostages Die in Attempted Missionary Rescue in Mindanao" in *Christianity Today* (July 8, 2002), 22.

3. Dave Busby, *The Heart of the Matter* (Grand Rapids: Full Court Press, 1993), 46.

4. Ibid., 47.

7 Hope

"Therefore, if anyone is in Christ, he is a new creation; the old has gone, the new has come! All this is from God" (2 Cor. 5:17-18). "I will never leave you nor forsake you" (Josh. 1:5).

Living Each Day to the Fullest

Everyone should be so lucky as to have a grandma like mine (Rachel's). She literally sings her "hello" when she answers the phone. Her hugs envelope you with love. At 92, she doesn't mind walking a mile to the beauty parlor, even though she still has her driver's license. She still heads the finance committee at church and is responsible for taking care of Sunday's offerings. She makes each of her nine grandchildren and 16 great-grandchildren feel special.

One of my favorite memories is helping Gram make Christmas cookies. Gram starts making cookies the day after Thanksgiving and she keeps baking until Christmas. In her heyday, Gram made 50 varieties of cookies for a total of more than 10,000 cookies one season.

When the cookies were done, we set up an assembly line, spreading tins of cookies on tables throughout the kitchen, dining room, and living room. Each grandkid grabbed a plastic tray and walked the line, filling it with cookies. At the end of the line, my mom or one of my aunts stood with cellophane to wrap the trays. Then a grandchild put a bow on the cellophane and declared the tray done. Completed trays were laid out in the family room to await delivery.

Over the holidays, Gram delivered her trays to "old people and shut-ins," many of whom were younger than she was! She wanted to touch these people, and a homemade gift was the best way she could do that.

What a wonderful tradition this is. Even better is the attitude that started the tradition in the first place and that keeps it going today. This is a labor of love for my grandmother. Her positive attitude made the real work of baking so many cookies and washing all those dishes fun.

When my grandpa died in 1992, Gram was again an inspiration. While the rest of us struggled to sing the hymns at his funeral, Gram sang beautifully. At the visitation the night before, she stood by the casket for hours, personally greeting everyone who came. Why wasn't she crying buckets like the rest of us? Wasn't she sad that Grandpa was gone? Sure she was. But her attitude that day was to celebrate his life and the more than 60 years they'd shared. The songs at his funeral were his favorites, so she sang them for him. I don't remember much of what the pastor said about my grandpa at the funeral. What sticks in my mind is the attitude my grandma chose for that day and most every day of her life—one of optimism and hope.

Optimism

Optimism is much like hope. According to Martin Seligman, professor of psychology at the University of Pennsylvania and author of *The Optimistic Child*, the basis of optimism lies in the way we think about causes.[1]

First, someone with an optimistic outlook sees bad events as temporary. There is hope that things can and will change. For example, if your family plans a weekend away together and something comes up so you have to cancel the trip, it can be terribly disappointing to stay home. Optimistic children, though disappointed, don't see whatever caused the cancellation happening again. There is hope of going on the trip at a later time.

Second, bad events are not contagious; they are contained to specific times and places. Rather than saying, "I can't do anything athletic!" an optimist will say, "I'm no good at gymnastics, but I can play soccer." Optimistic children don't generalize their weaknesses to include much more than is true.

Third, when bad events happen, optimistic children don't become mental victims. They don't completely blame them selves or others for what happened but rather are learning to take realistic responsibility for life's events.

Audrey had just gotten her license to drive. Feeling overconfident and in a hurry, she raced home to make her curfew. A police officer stopped her and issued her an $80 ticket. She was irate with the officer. In her mind, he should have been more sympathetic to her predicament. From her perspective, he was to blame.

Audrey had heard that police officers sometimes have a quota to fill—a certain number of tickets they have to write in a given time. She assumed that the officer who stopped her was just filling his quota and had no regard for her personal situation. She blamed the officer for stopping her and she blamed him for making her later than she already was. Audrey's assumptions were not only cynical, but they were also based on myth (the officer filling his quota) and speculation (her parents' reaction to her ticket and lateness).

Audrey is only 16, but she's already programmed her brain to have an initial negative reaction to bad situations. Her first reaction was anger and blame, followed by cynicism. In the same situation, an optimist might say, "I was speeding. I was wrong and deserved the ticket. I'll be more careful when I drive from now on." An optimist accepts responsibility for the situation and moves on with his or her life—water off a duck's back, as it were. Audrey will stew in her negative emotions for days.

Enemies of Hope: Depression and Cynicism

In 1996, 8,000 children under age six were using one of three commonly prescribed antidepressants: Prozac, Zoloft, or Paxil. Only one year later, that number rose 400 percent, to 40,000.[2] It would seem that depression is at epidemic proportions in both adults and children. How did that happen?

Dr. Seligman speculates social change has much to do with it.[3] Until 50 years ago, America was a nation of optimists. Our ancestors believed something better awaited them in America. They came hopeful, enduring great risk to settle here. Many found what they were looking for—freedom, opportunity, wealth—in spite of suffering great loss and hardship.

Following the Great Depression of the 1930s and the wars that followed, optimism lost its practicality. Americans were saddled with years of sorting through grief and loss. A turn toward pessimism ensued. And people wanted to feel good again.

Enter the self-esteem movement of the early 1960s. The humanistic efforts to move away from an achieving society and toward a feel-good society backfired. Programs intended to help kids believe that they were special and could become whatever they wanted weren't convincing. To tell a child he or she is "special" provokes skepticism if he or she doesn't understand it in context. To continually flatter someone without truthfully addressing his or her weaknesses is to create self-doubt and dependence, not bolster self-esteem. Such practices are not realistic and children know it.

The result was that we turned our focus inward. We are now experts on what we need and don't have. This absorption has contributed to a general lack of hope.

Between 1962 and 1998, the teenage suicide rate increased 134 percent.[4] Suicide is an option chosen by someone who has run out of hope. According to the Children's Defense Fund, "Every Day in America," six children and youth under age 20 commit suicide.[5] At some point, these children lost hope that their life situation would change. That's one of the key differences between optimism and pessimism: an optimist believes things can or will *change*.

According to Seligman, pessimists do worse than optimists in these ways:

- Pessimists are depressed more often.
- Pessimists achieve less at school, on the job, on the playing field.
- The physical health of a pessimist is worse than that of an optimist.[6]

A pessimist's mind-set bends toward the negative. Whether it's his or her circumstances or own personal traits the pessimist doesn't like, he or she feels somewhat powerless to change. The pessimist feels like a victim.

Cynics know the victim feeling too. They've been hurt, usually more than once. Perhaps a dream or an expectation was met with cold, harsh reality. Whatever the hurt, the by-product is cynicism to protect against getting hurt again. Cynics often are sarcastic. Their vulnerability hides behind words and phrases like "Whatever," "Yeah, right," and "I don't care." Although the cynic may be resigned in that way of thinking, a person swallowed up in cynicism says, "I dare you to give me hope. Get to my heart. Don't give up on me."

Time Out: Responding to Disappointment

Think about times when your children were disappointed. How did they respond? Did they have the optimistic qualities that preserved hope? How do you react to disappointment—with optimism or pessimism? Next time your children face disappointment, what will you do to encourage an optimistic response? Remember, everyone enjoys people who are realistically optimistic and hopeful about life. A positive attitude can be a safeguard against depression, and it can be learned!

Learned Hopefulness

When I (Rachel) am around my grandma, I'm inspired to look at life more optimistically. She has a positive attitude, even in bad circumstances. She puts others before herself and has a servant's heart. What a rich heritage she has given my family. Do you know someone like her? Make an effort to spend more time with that person and, if it's feasible, bring your children along. We all can learn from a positive example.

Your Child's Temperament

We can't overlook the fact that our inborn temperament type has something to do with our perspective on hope. Some of us have temperaments that are easily swayed to think negatively. Others are naturally more easygoing. Let's review the basic temperament types.[7]

Melancholy

A person with a Melancholy temperament is often moody. Usually these people have low self-esteem and are introverts. However, they are great thinkers, artistic, and creative. They tend to be perfectionists and are typically analytical. This is a setup for negative thinking. Melancholy persons must work harder at keeping their thoughts realistic and in check to maintain hope.

Choleric

Those with Choleric temperaments are highly independent, controlling, visionary, and successful. Though optimistic, Cholerics have their hope in themselves and what they can do. It's difficult for Cholerics to trust that someone else, including God, can do things as well as they can. Since Cholerics like to make deals, we can talk to them about what they will gain from putting their hope in God. But more times than not, they will learn this the hard way. That said, parents of Cholerics need God-given strength to approach their children rationally rather than emotionally.

Sanguine

The Sanguine temperament is also optimistic. Sanguines believe life is an exciting social experience that should be lived to the fullest. These folks are warm and see the good in other people. But they can be impulsive and undisciplined, and exaggerate their emotions. Sanguines are not easily discouraged. Because they put such a high value on relationships, they can learn to put their hope in people and God if they believe that others love and accept them. They are most responsive to love and adoration.

Supine

Those with Supine temperaments are relationship-oriented. They desire to serve others with an inborn gentle spirit. But they fear rejection, expect others to read their minds, and have trouble making decisions. They are not assertive and often feel at the mercy of others. Like Sanguines, Supines need to feel loved and accepted. They are responders, not initiators. It is not difficult for Supines to hope in others if they feel accepted or to hope in God if they feel His love, joy, and peace.

Phlegmatic

People with Phlegmatic temperaments are easygoing slow movers but are efficient and can persist at tedious tasks. They are stubborn and can be self-righteous. They *observe* life, relationships, and God rather than becoming *involved* because they are task-oriented. They want peace and tranquility. Their hope in God will bring rewards and benefit them. It's important for Phlegmatics to understand specifically how this will happen.

Do you see yourself or your child in any of these descriptions? Maybe you have a little of all of these. Maybe your child is more one than the other. As you explore temperament types, remember we're not trying to pigeonhole our children or put them in a temperament box. Let the insights you gain inform how you communicate with your child not serve as an excuse for bad behavior or miscommunication.

For more information about temperament, see the list of resources in Appendix C.

What Do You Think?

Since the basis of optimism and hope lies in the way we think, it's important to help children identify what they believe and think, as we talked about in chapter 4. Help them understand that they don't *have* to believe the first thing that pops into their minds. Take this example: Gerard's father was getting ready to leave on a business trip. Eleven-year-old Gerard was having trouble going to sleep the night before because he had thoughts of his father's plane crashing, of never seeing him again, of being terribly lonely without his father. These thoughts and fears are common among children. In such a case, teach your child to imagine capturing these fearful and negative thoughts and putting them in a cage. The visual image suggests that the child has some control over these intrusive thoughts, and you're giving your child a way to deal with them. The thoughts are prisoner to the child rather than vice versa. (See 2 Cor. 10:5.)

The next step is to evaluate how likely or true these thoughts are. An 11-year-old is capable of asking himself, "Is this true?" In Gerard's case, he had to admit it was possible that these events could happen. He needed to ask, "How *likely* is it that this will happen?" He needed help talking through probability—it is not likely his dad's plane will crash. Gerard thought about the many times Dad has returned safely from business trips. Gerard's mom used Scripture to reassure him that God is with his father wherever he goes. Gerard knows Scripture is true. When truth is held up against our fears, we are given hope.

Let's look at another example of changing thought patterns. Maggie feels left out at school and believes she has no friends. The thought she needs to capture and put in the cage is, "I have no friends." Next, it's time to evaluate if this is true. As Maggie thinks about it, she asks herself, "Is it true that *nobody* at school likes me?" She begins to picture different people who have been nice to her. She is not able to say that her belief is true. Maggie's parents are privy to her self-talk, so they encourage her by praising her friendly qualities. They also arrange a play date with another child her age to encourage one-on-one friendship building. Her parents are helping Maggie line her false belief up against the truth.

Believe in Your Child's Success

Helen Baumgartner believed in me (Pam). She was my college piano teacher. Helen could pull abilities out of me that I didn't know existed. She wasn't a cheerleader saying, "Come on, you can do it!" Instead, she showed me what she wanted, then pleasantly expected it from me. I'd watch her face and sense her attitude toward me. I could feel her hope in me. There was an emotional connection. And I wanted to please my teacher.

It was never more evident than when Helen took a sabbatical. My new teacher viewed teaching differently. She was a perfectionist with a serious demeanor. I sensed her expectation but didn't see her hope for me. That necessary emotional connection to motivate an insecure piano student was not there. Sad to say, I lost interest in taking lessons.

It's a form of grace to believe in the infinite possibilities of what God can and will do in your child's life, and then act on it. Grace doesn't allow present weaknesses to take focus; it looks at what we can become. Your child will more than likely live out a self-fulfilling prophecy with your encouragement.

Peter, Peter, Peter

Jesus' belief in Peter is a good example. Impetuous Peter denied Christ three times. Even before that happened, Jesus saw Peter for what he would become and loved him anyway! Peter is a vivid example of how God can change a person who follows Him. When Peter first started spending time with Jesus, he was impulsive, quick-tempered, unpredictable, and rough around the edges. Even near Jesus' death, Peter was behaving like—well, *Peter*. Jesus saw how these traits could be refined and used for good in Peter's life. He saw what Peter could become, and responded to him as a new creature in Christ by affirming him:

[Jesus asked His disciples,] "Who do men say that I am?" Peter responded emphatically, "You are the Christ, the Messiah, the Son of the living God." To this Jesus replied, "God bless you, Simon, son of Jonah! You didn't get that answer from books or from teachers. My Father in Heaven, God Himself, let you in on the secret of Who I really am. And now I'm going to tell you who you really are. You are Peter, a rock. This is the rock on which I will put together my church, a church so expansive with energy that not even the gates of Hell will be able to keep it out" *(Matt. 16:16-18, TM)*.

This message of hope included Peter's value to God. Peter wasn't perfect, but God planned to do great things through him. Peter needed to hear this. He probably needed it most after the rooster crowed.

In the same way, our children will soak up our hope for them. Whether we show it in our attitude or with words as well, it will be as fertilizer on a young plant to help it become strong and beautiful.

Spiritual Implications

We gain hope from experiencing God's grace. Hope is based on our perception of who God is and how He feels about us. Like trust for someone, it builds over time as we notice Him work and experience His kindness.

A pessimist might say, "A good God does not exist. Look at all the evil things that happen in this world." The pessimist does not understand or notice the ways of God and is not able to reconcile the evil in the world with the supposedly good character of God. Thus, the pessimist generalizes God is not good or doesn't exist. On the contrary, a person with the hope of God would say, "I can't explain completely why bad things happen to good people. But I know that God has been kind to me in many instances. Not everything goes as I have planned, but I have experienced God's goodness."

A hopeful person who knows the salvation of Jesus Christ can worship God even when bad events happen. He or she doesn't view God as the cause but rather as the One who will bring good. Consider Paul's words to the Romans: "And we know that in all things God works for the good of those who love him, who have been called according to his purpose" (8:28).

We often confuse this verse to mean that God will make sure everything in our life is "good" by our definition. If you define "good" as having a large house, two cars, plenty of money in the bank, and no health problems, you could be in for a bit of a surprise if you assume Rom. 8:28 promises that God will hand you these things. Look at the verse again: "In all things *God works for the good of those who love him.*" He promises a rainbow. Noah had to live through the Flood, but there was a pretty nifty rainbow at the end of it. And remember Joseph's wise words to his brothers? "You intended to harm me, but God intended it for good to accomplish what is now being done, the saving of many lives" (Gen. 50:20).

We have hope not because we know God will keep bad things from happening to us but because we know He will help us persevere through them. It's hard not to say, "Why me, Lord?" and instead ask, "What would You have me learn from this, Lord? What is Your plan for me?"

It was not even one week after my (Pam's) son, Mike, got his driver's license. I happened to be talking to my husband in his office. The phone rang; it was our son. He had been in a car accident 20 minutes away. Randy and I jumped in the car. As we drove to the scene, the ambulance and sheriff's vehicles were just ahead of us. We only knew that Mike and the others involved were shaken but alive.

When we got to the scene, Mike was sitting in the ambulance with a neck brace on, head in his hands, weeping quietly. His passenger was also in the ambulance with minor injuries. Mike had crossed the highway intersection too quickly and didn't see a car in his blind spot traveling 60 mph. Both cars were totaled. The driver of the other car sustained minor injuries. We were all emotionally moved, thinking of what could have happened. That feeling of vulnerability bothered me tremendously.

The next morning, I asked God to speak to me through His Word. I randomly opened my Bible to Ps. 68:19-20 (NLT): "Praise the Lord; praise God our savior! For each day he carries us in his arms. Our God is a God who saves! The Sovereign LORD rescues us from death."

I can't explain why some people die in car crashes and others survive. But I do know that God ordains all the days of our lives (Ps. 139:16). It was clear to me that God chose to save our son, his friend, and an innocent driver from death that day—evidence of His grace. I was to praise Him for His protection and not ruminate on how I could have been planning a funeral. I shifted my thinking and verbally began to testify to others of God's watchful care. My worship of God has been impacted. It's more meaningful because my gratitude and my hope in Christ have substance. Without hope in Him, we are left to ourselves and our fears.

Teaching Hope

Children need a sense of spirituality. It's part of who we are. A hope in God satisfies a child's preoccupation with fearful emotions and the hard questions like: What happens when people die? How can God communicate with us when we can't see Him? What about the unexplainable?

With questions like these, children are ripe to have us teach them about God. They are hungry, imaginative, and impressionable. When children learn that God created them, gave them to parents who will love and care for them, and is "big" enough to take them to a safe place like heaven when they die, they feel more secure. Children want and need to know that God is loving and powerful beyond all else. How do we make these truths sink in?

If your children are age seven or younger, use stories to re-solve the fears and emotional tension generated by violent im-ages they receive from media and their imagination. You might try biblical stories like Jesus and the children (Matt. 19:13-14; Mark 9:36-37; 10:13-16), the Flood (Gen. 7:1—8:22), David and Goliath (1 Sam. 17), and Jesus' resurrection (Matt. 28:1-20; Mark 16:1-20; Luke 24:1-53) that provide resolution and victory. Other stories like Joseph (Gen. 37:1—50:26) illustrate that sometimes it takes many years for good to win out in bad situa-tions, but God will prevail. These stories provide hope in the love and power of God.

For preschoolers, you might use children's Bibles or Bible story books and picture books to tell these stories as the biblical accounts are quite graphic. The stabbing and beheading of Go-liath in 1 Sam. 17 for example is more than a 3-year-old needs to hear. See Appendix D for a list of good resources.

Older children from ages 8 to 12 have trouble with abstract concepts like *grace.* For them, broken rules require punishment —cut and dried. Children this age who have the extra saddle of guilt often deal with feelings of inadequacy and believe they aren't good enough to merit God's grace or to go to heaven un-less they earn it. Although this age-group relates to the Law of the Old Testament, they don't understand the true meaning and purpose of God's "rules." They are aware of and worried about world problems such as national and international security, war, and famine. To teach children this age, try stories like Gideon (Judg. 6:1—8:35) and Daniel (Dan. 6:1-28) and others that em-phasize God's omnipotence. These stories reinforce the concept that God preserves and saves us.

Teenagers are, in general, conformists. They may act like they want to be different, but secretly they need to feel accepted and affirmed. They are often self-conscious and aware of their own limitations and weaknesses. For them, hope comes from know-ing that God accepts and loves them and that He can change them. He promises to make them new creatures as they submit to Him. As teens struggle to figure out who they are and what they like, they are bound to make mistakes. For them we recom-mend stories like Rahab (Josh. 2:1-24; 5:13—6:27), David (2

Sam. 11:1—12:31), Peter (Matt. 14:22-3?; 16:21-28; 26:31-75), and Paul (Acts 9:1-31; 13:1—28:31) and other personal testimonies that emphasize God's love and forgiveness.

Without hope in God, we are left to rely on ourselves. That's a scary thought. We know we can't control whether Saddam Hussein or Osama bin Laden begin a chemical war. We know we can't protect our children and grandchildren every moment. Without hope in God, there is justifiable fear. But with hope, we can remain relatively steadfast. And for examples of those unswayed by fear, we can look to the faith hall of famers like Moses and his parents. Moses' parents were not gripped with fear by the king's decree to kill the Hebrew baby boys (Heb. 11:23). In fact, the Bible says they were "unawed." When Moses was born, his parents knew in their hearts that God would find a way to protect their baby for His purpose. It was their hope and faith in God that kept their emotions in check.

And when Moses left Egypt, he was not afraid of what the king could do to him for leaving without explanation. He knew his purpose was eventually to lead Israel out of bondage, so he held to that goal without fear of his circumstances (Heb. 11:24-29).

Then there's Abraham with his checkered past, sometimes demonstrating great hope and faith in God, sometimes falling on his face. On more than one occasion, he felt he needed to deceive Pharaoh and the king, telling them Sarah was his sister so his own life would be spared. He worked hard on his own behalf. But God didn't give up on him when he made mistakes. Abraham passed the ultimate test of hope in God when he was asked to sacrifice his only son.

Abraham and Sarah waited many years to have a child. Their son, Isaac, was their delight, their life. When Isaac was an adolescent, God came to Abraham with another opportunity to trust Him. God asked Abraham to take his only son, Isaac, his long-awaited heir, and sacrifice him as a burnt offering (Gen. 22:1-19). So he obeyed. He rose early in the morning to get ready. Abraham must have been clinging to the promises God had made to him about having descendants as numerous as the dust of the earth (13:16).

Isaac must have wondered why his dad asked him to climb

up on the altar and allow himself to be tied to the kindling. No doubt Isaac realized what was happening, but he trusted his father as Abraham trusted God.

Knife raised, Abraham was ready to slay his own son out of obedience to God. But the Lord called urgently to Abraham to stop. A ram was stuck in the thicket nearby. It would become Abraham's sacrifice. Abraham's test was over. God knew his heart. Abraham had put God first, even above his own son. And once again, Abraham saw God provide. What incredible intimacy Abraham must have felt with God at that moment! God, so pleased with His faithful servant's obedience, saw the emotional and physical sacrifice Abraham made to trust Him. And Abraham experienced the audible affirmation and blessing of God commending him for trusting and hoping. The tone of God's voice conveyed a love unfathomably deep. And there were blessings yet to come. Abraham would be the father of children as numerous as the stars and his would be the family line for the Messiah. Words can't describe that holy, intimate moment with God.

Our faith and hope in Jesus Christ allows us to control (to some degree) hard-to-manage emotions like fear and anger. But even more, our hope in God's goodness makes obedience an intimate blessing.

Chapter 7 Endnotes

1. Martin Seligman, *The Optimistic Child* (New York: Houghton Mifflin Company, 1995), 52.

2. Empower.org. "Depressing Numbers," *Washington Times.* May 30, 1999, cited in *Index of Leading Cultural Indicators 2001,* 165.

3. Seligman, *Optimistic Child,* 40.

4. Empower.org, 130.

5. Nelson and Cowan, *100 Harshest Facts About Our Future.* Generation X Coalition, Inc.

6. Seligman, *Optimistic Child,* 51.

7. Richard Arno and Phyllis Arno, *Creation Therapy* (Sarasota, Fla.: Sarasota Academy of Christian Counseling, 1983).

8 Intimacy with God

"My heart has heard you say, 'Come and talk with me.' And my heart responds, 'LORD, I am coming'" (Ps. 27:8, NLT).
"We love Him, because He first loved us" (1 John 4:19, AMP.).

My daughter, Hannah, and I (Pam) went to spend a couple days with my parents before she headed back to college. Like many Minnesotans in the summertime, my parents spend time on a lake. So Hannah and I had planned to do some fishing with Grandpa. There's nothing like being out in a boat together for hours. It's quiet, there are no distractions, no pressure to make conversation. But the golden opportunity to get to know Grandpa was ours if we wanted it.

Retirement changes people. Dad is different since he sold his business. He has mellowed considerably and seems to enjoy doing more of the things he only had snippets of time to do when he was working.

Without the stress of work, his true nature came to light. And I wanted to know this person. We settled in a shallow spot off a buoyed area. Hannah sat in the back of the boat, Dad in the middle, and I in the front. We had everything we needed—minnows, leaches, and worms for bait to catch fish. How did my father know that I didn't want to touch any of those things? My idea of fishing was to hold the pole and reel 'em in. That's it!

In the several hours we spent fishing with my dad, he was a busy man. He baited our hooks and took off our fish while we sat back and thoroughly enjoyed the experience. He didn't complain or make us feel like we should do it ourselves. He was a servant. I saw his selflessness in helping us. And I was touched by his kindness. I recognized his love in action and, in turn, it encouraged the bond between us.

Suppose I had taken his actions for granted—not noticed the sacrifice he was making so fishing was more enjoyable for me and Hannah. I would have lost out on an emotional connection with him. I wouldn't have known I was receiving a blessing. And I certainly wouldn't have had any appreciation or affirmation. The intimate moment with my father *depended* on my response.

It's not much different with our Heavenly Father. The intimate moments with Jesus come when we are *touched* by His kindness, when we *recognize* the different ways He loves us and then *respond* to Him. Maybe it's a Scripture passage that diminishes a fear you face. It could be encouragement from a friend. It could be a divine moment where in your spirit you *know* that God cares about the things you care about. First it's recognized, then it's appreciated. These experiences build the emotional attachment between us and God.

When I (Pam) began to recognize the love and kindness of Jesus, my outlook on life changed. It's in the intimate moments with Jesus that we hear Him say, "I love you." Indeed, it was hearing those words in my spirit that began to change me. We can hear others say, "God loves you," but it pales in comparison to hearing it from God himself. As one friend put it, "We need more than a theory of God's love; each of us needs to experience it for ourselves."

"I love you" comes differently to each of us. I (Pam) asked several Christians how they would describe intimacy with God. One person said very simply, "Making a connection with God." This is a rather broad statement, but we know what it means if we've experienced some depth in relationships with our spouse or friends. Intimacy is being keenly familiar with Him and He with you, much to the joy and delight of both. A sacred romance, if you will, that involves a deep and secret inner exchange between God and us.

Another friend described intimacy as "a conscious awareness of God's protective care." Still another said she consistently goes to God with hope that she will experience closeness with Him even though it doesn't always happen. Sometimes He seems silent, but she waits.

Others listed ways they respond to God, such as spending time alone praying, meditating, reading, listening, and singing. These behaviors can be spontaneous or disciplined responses to God's love. But without having *experienced* God's love, these behaviors are empty, even legalistic.

Still others listed the effects of intimacy like a greater sense of peace, comfort, hope, care, and trust.

King David describes intimacy with God in Ps. 27:4 (AMP.). He says it's the one thing he seeks most—to live in the house of the Lord, gazing upon the beauty (the sweet attractiveness and the delightful loveliness) of the Lord and to meditate, consider, and inquire in His temple. David felt safe there. It was a refuge from his physical, emotional, and spiritual afflictions. He expressed his dependence upon God and longed to hear from Him —His wisdom, comfort, and guidance. He was open to letting God teach him how to live honestly. His hope was in God's goodness as he waited patiently for the Lord.

Hearing God say "I love you" is the first step in making an intimate connection with Him. The next step is our response. When we help our children develop emotional competence, we are helping them respond to others and to God like King David did.

King David's response? He subjected himself to God's authority, he waited, he knew what he needed, and he communicated it to God. He was aware of God's love for him. He responded with appreciation, and his hope was in God's deliverance.

David describes the effects of his response as being on a high rock where he was unaffected by the turmoil going on around him. His confidence and integrity were steadfast because he experienced God's love for him. Certainly, the experience was both rational and emotional. We want the same for our children and ourselves. Paradoxically, David's dependent response is what made him strong in spirit.

Strong in Spirit

To be strong in spirit suggests a mental disposition that uses wisdom and grace in relating to others. Those who are strong in spirit have an ability to use emotions for their good purpose while keeping them subject to the truth.

Samuel, John the Baptist, and Jesus are described as being strong in spirit (1 Sam. 2:26; Luke 1:80; 2:52). All three were set apart among men and found favor with God. They were strong physically as well as emotionally and mentally for God's purposes.

All three put themselves under the leadership of God. They had the discipline to deny their own creature comforts for the sake of their mission. They spent time alone with God communicating and getting direction. No doubt they received encouragement to keep going. They empathized with the people they served: healing, saving, ministering to, weeping with, evangelizing. They used their emotional and social competence to influence many and to stay connected to their Father. All three died with the hope and knowledge that they had fulfilled a purpose and would see God.

Although our role is necessary, parents can only do so much to help develop that kind of inner strength in their children. We can introduce our children to Christ and teach them the seven emotional skills. But it is the Holy Spirit who completes the work of making us strong in spirit. He helps us understand some of the mystery and truth about God and how He feels about us. He loves, comforts, helps, reveals, convicts, gives power, leads, gives gifts, stirs, quickens, gives life, refreshes, ministers, dwells, seals, strengthens, renews, teaches, justifies, and sanctifies. The good news is that the Spirit of God is given to each one of us who respond to God's invitation to become His child through His forgiveness. It's a form of grace unmatched on earth.

Our response to that grace is crucial. It's what perpetuates intimacy.

Responding to Grace

Intimacy happens when two parties respond to each other.

There's ebb and flow. There's graceful movement in the relationship on emotional and spiritual levels.

However, if one party refuses to respond or goes a different direction, the connection is lost. It becomes impossible to move together. If we overlook the kindness of others, we fail to perpetuate the relationship through appreciation and affirmation.

I (Pam) have talked about the grace my dad showed me in being a servant. I had to recognize it as something I didn't deserve from him—a gift—in order to appreciate it. How do we recognize and respond to God's grace? The awareness of our sin opens the door to grace and freedom. When we first recognize how much distance is between God and us because of sin and then realize what He did to bridge that gap, we get a glimpse of grace. Instead, many of us busy ourselves with proper behavior that covers up our sin. We look great on the outside but are empty on the inside. We miss out on being able to appreciate what God has done to be close to us. Philip Yancey, in his book *What's So Amazing About Grace,* says, "If we comprehend what Christ has done for us, then surely out of gratitude we will strive to live 'worthy' of such great love. We will strive for holiness not to make God love us but because he already does."[1]

The seven skills we've discussed in this book are powerful tools in your Christian parenting arsenal. And you'll need an arsenal because you've got lots of forces working against you. With these skills comes freedom—to find favor with others and a satisfying closeness with God.

Parenting can sometimes feel like a heavy weight. You won't be perfect because the perfect human parent does not exist. That's OK because Christianity is about restoration. God can take our mistakes and use them to make Christianity real and appealing to our children. We can model for our children repentant sinners who have received grace. And our wonderful God uses our mistakes to show our children how to connect with Him.

It's in that connection that worship becomes meaningful. We show God our appreciation and we affirm what we know Him to be, what He has saved us from, and the freedom He has given us. Worship is our response to Him because we've experienced His grace in our lives.

Scripture Prayers for Our Children

You can see from the examples of biblical parenting presented in Scripture that God used imperfect people for His perfect purposes. This includes those He chose to parent the leaders of His kingdom. And He does the same today.

Though we make mistakes, we do the best we can to introduce the most precious people in our lives to Jesus. Once they meet the Savior, a relationship begins that will be influenced by many things. But the most influential force in directing their walk will be supernatural—the work of the Holy Spirit and your prayers.

Here are some prayers directly from Scripture that you can pray for the people you love.

Dear Lord, I pray that You will pour out Your Spirit and Your blessing on [child's name]. May she thrive like watered grass, like willows on a riverbank. And may she proudly claim, "I belong to the Lord." Amen (Isa. 44:3-4).

Dear Lord, I pray that from Your glorious, unlimited resources You will give [child's name] mighty inner strength through Your Holy Spirit. And I pray that Christ will be more and more at home in his heart as he trusts in You. May his roots go down deep into the soil of Your marvelous love. And may he have the power to understand how wide, how long, how high, and how deep Your love really is. May he *experience* the love of Christ, though it is so great he will never fully understand it. Then he will be filled with the fullness of life and power that comes from You. Now glory be to God! By Your mighty power at work within us, You are able to accomplish infinitely more than we would ever dare to ask or hope. May You be given glory in the church and in Christ Jesus forever and ever through endless ages. Amen (Eph. 3:16-21).

Dear Lord, I will keep asking that You, God of our Lord Jesus Christ, the glorious Father, may give [child's name] the spirit of wisdom and revelation, so that she may know Christ better. I pray also that the eyes of [child's name]'s heart may be enlightened, in order that she may know the hope to which You have called her, the riches of Your glorious inheritance in the saints, and Your incomparable great power for us who believe. Amen (Eph. 1:17-20).

Dear Lord, I pray that [child's name] may be encouraged in heart and united in love, so that he may have the full riches of complete understanding, in order that he may know the mystery of God, namely Christ, in whom are hidden all treasures of wisdom and knowledge. Amen (Col. 2:2-3).

Dear Lord, I pray that [child's name]'s love may abound more and more in knowledge and depth of insight, so that she may be able to discern what is best and may be pure and blameless until the day of Christ, filled with the fruit of righteousness that comes through Jesus Christ—to the glory and praise of God Amen (Phil. 1:9-11).

Dear Lord, I pray that the grace of the Lord Jesus Christ will be with [child's name]'s spirit. Amen (Phil. 4:23).

These prayers are for blessing our children's lives. A blessing is powerful. It heals, builds, gives life, nurtures, and gives strength. And prayer is the road to intimacy with God. A speaker friend of mine (Pam's) says when he looks out into an audience of young people, he can "see" the kids whose parents pray for them. We can't control what happens to our children, but we _can_ pray for them. What a wonderful tool God has given us.

Being a Christian parent is one of the most powerful and influential positions on earth. May God bless you as you impact the world as a parent.

Chapter 8 Endnotes

1. Phillip Yancey, _What's So Amazing About Grace?_ (Grand Rapids: Zondervan, 1997), 190.

Appendix A

Resources to Help with Establishing Authority

If you feel you and your child need guidance in establishing a healthy respect for authority, don't be afraid to ask for help. Focus on the Family (1-800-A FAMILY) has a list of Christian counselors in your state who could help. Also, the American Association of Christian Counselors (1-800-5-COUNSEL) can share the names and numbers of its members in your area of the country. Check with your local public school district. Does its early childhood education program offer assistance for parents? (If you live in Missouri or Kansas, ask your school district about the Parents as Teachers program. If you live in Minnesota, ask for Early Childhood and Family Education classes for parents and children.) There are also numerous web sites with Christian parenting information that you can access by typing "Christian Parenting" into a search engine. Here are some good ones:

Train Up a Child in the Way He Should Go—Dr. William Sears presents a primer on Christian parenting.
http://www.mothering.com/SpecialArticles/Issue93/FAMLIV.html

Rocky Mountain Family Council—a nonprofit organization advocating for Christian parenting. http://www.rmfc.org/

Christian Single Parents—a guide to single parenting for those of the Christian faith, featuring topics like finances and budgets.
http://www.christiansingleparentsonline.com/

711.NET Christian Chat Network—large Christian community with chat rooms and message boards. http://www.711webcafe.net/

FaithMD—advice on parenting and marriage from Christian pastors, scholars, and counselors; includes a newsletter published by John Tesh. http://www.faithmd.com/

Christianity Today on Parenting—connecting today's Christian families with practical and biblical advice and with one another.
http://www.christianitytoday.com/parenting/

Appendix B

Resources to Teach Your Children About Finances

There are a number of resources to help us teach children (starting at preschool age) how to manage money wisely. Here are some of our favorites.

Blue, Ron, and Judy Blue. *Raising Money-Smart Kids: How to Teach Your Children the Secrets of Earning, Saving, Investing, and Spending Wisely.* Nashville: Thomas Nelson, 1992. This book has limited availability from www.amazon.com.

Burkett, Larry, and Marnie Wooding. *Money Matters for Teens.* Chicago: Moody Press, 1998. For more information on "Money Matters" titles for all ages, go to www.moodypress.com and click on "finances."

Godfrey, Neale S., and Carolina Edwards. *Money Doesn't Grow on Trees: A Parent's Guide to Raising Financially Responsible Children.* New York: Fireside, 1994. *New York Times* No. 1 Best-Seller. For more information on Neale Godfrey, a noted speaker and expert on family finances, go to www.eaglestalent.com. Click on "search database," then type in her name. According to the *New York Times,* Neale is "The Brazelton of family finance."

Godfrey, Neale S. *Neale S. Godfrey's Ultimate Kids' Money Book.* New York: Simon and Schuster, 1998.

McCurrach, David. *Kids' Allowances—How Much, How Often and How Come: A Guide for Parents.* Franklin, Tenn.: Kids Money Press, 2000. Includes allowance workbook. For more information, go to www.kidsmoneypress.com.

www.thegoodsteward.com. This web site offers a bevy of financial information.

Appendix C

Resources on Temperament Types

There are a number of books and programs devoted to exploring different temperament types. Here are the ones we've found most helpful:

Arno, Richard, and Phyllis Arno. *The Arno Profile System.* This system is a 54-question test measuring inborn temperament with an accuracy rate of 95.7 percent. The APS is available through certified biblical counselors or individuals who have taken the Arnos' Creation Therapy course. The premise of the Arnos' work is that we are created in God's image and our temperaments are God-given. Knowing our temperament type helps us understand why we do the very things we do not want to do, what causes inner conflicts and conflicts with others, and what our hidden needs as unique individuals are. For more information, contact the Sarasota Academy of Christian Counseling, 3650 17th St., Sarasota, FL 34235, or call 941-951-6834 or visit their web site at www.APSReport.com.

Littauer, Florence, and Marita Littauer. *Personality Plus for Parents.* Available through the authors' website, www.classervices.com or from CLASServices Inc., P.O. Box 66810, Albuquerque, NM 87193. 1-800-433-6633. The Littauers also provide other resources on the same topic, including a fact sheet called "Understanding Children's Personalities."

Smalley, Gary, and John Trent. *Homes of Honor.* Dr. Smalley is one of America's foremost speakers on family relationships. This program includes videotapes, a workbook, and a hardcover book, teaching parents to communicate more effectively with their children. For more information, go to www.smalleyonline.com or www.garysmalleyvideos.com.

Appendix D

Children's Books and Bibles

Check with your local Christian bookstore to find age-appropriate books that will help you teach your children Bible stories and biblical values. Here are some of our favorites:

Brown, Jennifer. *Hooray! It's a Duck Day!* (St. Louis: Concordia Publishing House, 1998). In this delightful picture book, Nana shows her granddaughter, Emily, that God works for her good, even when disappointing things happen.

Currie, Robin. *Toddlers' Action Bible.* (St. Louis: Concordia Publishing House, 1998). The interactive Bible stories in this book help toddlers learn about their loving Savior.

Hastings, Selina. *The Children's Illustrated Bible.* (New York: Dorling Kindersley, 1994). These are short one- to two-page rewritten stories from the Bible with beautiful illustrations by Eric Thomas.

Henley, Karyn. *The Beginner's Bible.* (Grand Rapids: Zonderkidz, 1997). This popular book retells favorite Bible stories in language young children can easily understand.

Lucado, Max. *Just in Case You Ever Wonder.* (Dallas: WordKids, 1992.) A parent tells a child just how precious he or she is to God and to his or her parents.

Tangvald, Christine. *Tuck Me In, God.* (St. Louis: Concordia Publishing House, 1998.) This wonderful bedtime book helps children tell God about all the events, places, and people in their day.

Build Your Marriage to Complete, Not Compete

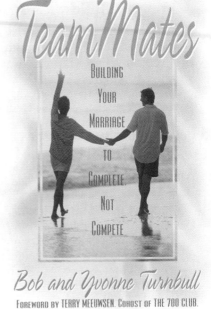

HUSBANDS AND WIVES often pray the same prayer, separately, "Lord, why didn't You make us more similar? That way my life could be so much easier." Because of their differences, spouses often struggle against each other when marital problems arise. They miscommunicate, become frustrated, angry, or resentful. But God has a greater plan for a husband and wife and by design, He created us to come together as one.

TeamMates

BUILDING
YOUR
MARRIAGE
TO
COMPLETE
NOT
COMPETE

Bob and Yvonne Turnbull

FOREWORD BY TERRY MEEUWSEN. COHOST OF THE 700 CLUB.

BFZZ083-411-7177

Marriage speakers Bob and Yvonne Turnbull bring their singular sense of humor and unique presentation to the page, training couples to work as a team. They travel the country full-time, presenting Celebration Seminars, which apply biblical principles to marriages and families.